the forbidden rainbow

IMAGES AND VOICES FROM LATIN AMERICA

the forbidden rainbow

IMAGES AND VOICES FROM LATIN AMERICA

photographs by julio etchart • edited by amanda hopkinson

Library of Congress Catalog Card Number: 92-60148

British Library Cataloguing in Publication Data

Etchart, Julio
Forbidden Rainbow: Images from Latin America
I. Title II.Hopkinson, Amanda
779

ISBN 1-85242 261 0

Introduction by Eduardo Galeano first published in *We Say No*,
W.W. Norton, New York, 1992.

'The White Wall and the Spider' by Daniel Moyano is taken
from *After the Despots*, by Andrew Graham-Yooll,
Bloomsbury Publishing Ltd., London, 1991

First published 1992 by Serpent's Tail
4 Blackstock Mews, London N4 and
401 West Broadway #2, New York, NY 10012

Design by Fiona Keating
Typeset in 10/14pt Aster by Bookman, Bristol
Printed in Great Britain by Longdunn Press, Bristol

contents

980.03
E83

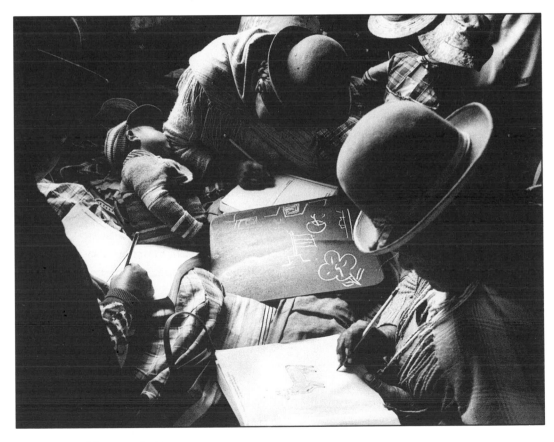

acknowledgments

Many people shared their time with me and gave assistance over the many years during which these pictures were taken.

I owe a special debt to my spouse Linda for her advice, as well as emotional and practical support. Our son Alex cheered me up when the going got tough. Kristin Vrengdenhil kept him entertained.

I am grateful to Carlos Guarita and Lucy Goodison; my partners at Reportage Photos for their constructive criticism, and to my colleagues at Impact Visuals in New York for their encouragement.

To Pete Ayrton for his adventurous spirit; Fiona Keating for her design skills; John Hampson for his attention to detail and patience. And also Deirdre Clark, Jean McNeil and Gaby Naher at Serpent's Tail.

My thanks to Mo Fini of Tumi for his insight and specialist knowledge; to Louis Byrne, Simon Fisher and Cristina Sganga for their hospitality and advice. To Diana Mansfield from the BBC and film maker Patricio Guzmán for providing me with background material; Sister Anselm Gunn and Father Liam Holoham for their hospitality and spiritual comfort.

I would also like to thank the following individuals and organisations: Luis Silva and War on Want; Anne Chaplin, Liz Clayton, Geoff Sayer and Christine Whitehead at Oxfam; CIIR, and the Latin America Bureau.

Last, but not least, thanks to Amanda Hopkinson for bringing this project together.

Julio Etchart, London, May 1992.

I would like to dedicate these images to the
memory of my parents, Maria T. Lenoble and
Julio C. Etchart.

Julio Etchart was born in Montevideo, Uruguay in 1950. He moved to France in 1974, and then to England, where he has lived since 1976. He regularly contributes photographs to newspapers and magazines such as *The Guardian*, *The Sunday Times*, *New Internationalist*, *The Observer*, *Der Spiegel*, *Libération*, and *Cambio-16*, and his work has featured in many books, including *The Latin Americans* (BBC Publications). Julio Etchart is a co-founder of Reportage Photos (London) and a member of Impact Visuals (New York).

Amanda Hopkinson, who was born in London, is a specialist in Latin American studies. Currently editor of the human rights magazine *Central America Report*, she has edited and translated a number of books, including *They Won't Take Me Alive*, *Family Album* and *Lovers and Comrades*.

introduction

the forbidden rainbow

EDUARDO GALEANO

The Discovery. On 12 October 1492, America discovered capitalism. Christopher Columbus, financed by the king and queen of Spain and the bankers of Genoa, introduced this novelty to the islands of the Caribbean. In his annals of the Discovery, the Admiral wrote the word *gold* 139 times and *Our Lord* or *God* 51 times. His eyes never tired of seeing such beauty in those golden beaches, and on 27 November he prophesied: 'All Christendom will find commerce here.' In this he was not mistaken. Columbus thought that Haiti was Japan, Cuba was China, and that the inhabitants of Japan and China were the Indians of India. But concerning commerce Columbus was not mistaken.

By the end of five centuries of Christian commerce, one third of American woodlands have been destroyed, much formerly fertile ground is now barren, and over half the entire population feeds on scraps. The Indians, victims of the greatest plunder in the world's history, are still suffering from the usurpation of their residual lands, condemned to the denial of a separate identity. They remain forbidden to live according to traditional ways and customs, without the right *to be*. At the start, the looting and the *othercide* were conducted in the name of God and His Heavens. Today the god of Progress has taken over.

Despite everything, in the midst of this banned and devalued identity, there still glimmer clues to another possible America, that America, blinded by racism, cannot discern.

On 12 October 1492, Columbus noted in his log that he intended to transport Indians back home 'so that they might learn to speak' [que deprenden fablar]. Five centuries later, on 12 October 1989, a court in the United States declared a Mixteco Indian 'mentally retarded' for failing to speak fluent Spanish: Ladislao Pastrana, an Oaxacan Mexican working illegally in California as a cropper, was to be locked up in a state asylum for life. Pastrana was unable to understand his Spanish interpreter and the court psychologist diagnosed 'evident mental deficiency'. Finally the anthropologists shed light on the matter: Pastrana expressed himself perfectly in his own language, Mixteca, as spoken by the Indian descendants of a high culture with a history going back over 2,000 years.

The language of Paraguay is Guaraní. A case unique in world history: the language of the Indians, of the vanquished, is the undisputed national language. Notwithstanding, according to polls taken, a majority of Paraguayans consider that anyone who doesn't understand Spanish is 'an animal'.

One Peruvian in every two is Indian, and the Peruvian

Constitution declares Quechua an official language on a par with Spanish. The Constitution says so, but reality isn't listening. Peru treats its Indians as South Africa treats its blacks. Only Spanish is taught in school, and is the language of the country's judges, police and officials. (Spanish is not, however, the only language on television since television also speaks English.)

Five years ago, Buenos Aires' civil registrars refused to register the birth of a child. The parents, indigenous to the north-eastern province, wanted their son to be called Qori Wamancha, a Jujuy name. The Argentine registrar refused to accept it on the grounds that 'the name was a foreign one'.

American Indians are exiles in their own land. Their languages are not a mark of identity but a curse, not a distinguishing feature but an accusation. When Indians surrender their languages they begin to become civilised. To become civilised or to commit suicide?

When I was a schoolchild in Uruguay, we were taught that Uruguay had been saved from the *indigenous problem* thanks to the nineteenth-century generals who exterminated the last native Uruguayans.

The indigenous problem: the first Americans, the true discoverers of America, are a *problem*. In order for the problem to stop being a problem, Indians have to cease being Indians. Erase them from the map, or erase their soul. Annihilate or assimilate. Genocide or othercide.

In December 1976, the Brazilian Interior Minister triumphantly proclaimed 'the Indian problem would be completely resolved' by the end of the twentieth century. Then every Indian would be properly integrated into Brazilian society and no longer be an Indian. The minister explained that the organisation officially dedicated to their protection (FUNAI, the Fundacao Nacional do Indio) would assume responsibility for their civilisation, or rather for their disappearance. Bullets, dynamite, gifts of poisoned food, contaminated rivers, the destruction of the forests, and the spread of viruses and bacteria previously unknown to Indians have accompanied the invasion of the Amazon basin by companies anxious to exploit minerals, timber and other resources. Even such an extensive and ferocious onslaught has not sufficed. The domestication of the scarce Indian survivors *to protect them from barbarism* is one more indispensable weapon in the removal of any obstacle in the way of conquest.

'Kill the Indian and save the man,' advised the pious North American Colonel Henry Pratt. Many years later, the Peruvian novelist Mario Vargas Llosa is explaining that there is no alternative to the modernisation of Indians, even if this means sacrificing their cultures, in order to save them from hunger and destitution.

Salvation condemns Indians to work from dawn to dark in mines and on plantations, for a daily rate that wouldn't cover the cost of a tin of dogfood. *Saving* the Indians also includes breaking up their communal sanctuaries and forcing them to sell cheap hand-thrown pottery on violent city streets, where they trade in their languages, their names and their clothes to end up as beggars or drunks or working in whorehouses. Or else *saving* Indians consists in putting them into uniform and sending them off, rifles at their shoulder, to kill other Indians or else to die defending the system that denies them. When the chips are down, Indians serve as good cannon-fodder: out of 25,000 North American Indians sent to the Second World War, 10,000 died.

On 16 December 1492, Columbus recorded that Indians are useful 'under orders and compelled to work, sowing and performing whatever tasks were deemed necessary, thus may they move into towns and adapt to our clothes and customs'. Cooption of labour, theft of the soul; the name of the game from the start of colonisation and throughout the Americas comes from the verb *to diminish*. A *saved* Indian is a *diminished* Indian. To diminish to the point of disappearance. Emptied of their selves, Indians become non-Indians and no-bodies.

The Paraguayan Chamacoco shaman sings to the stars, to the spiders and to mad Totila, who wanders weeping through the forest. He relays the song of the kingfisher: 'Suffer not the pangs of hunger and thirst. Mount my wings and together we'll eat fish from the river and drink the wind.'

He relays the tale told by the mists: 'I come to dispel the frost, lest your people suffer from cold.'

And he relays the refrain of the winged horses: 'Mount and let us ride in search of the rain.'

But evangelical missionaries obliged the shaman to abandon his plumes, his bells and his incantations as *instruments of the devil*, and no more may he heal snakebites, summon the rain during the dry season nor fly over the land singing of what he sees. In an interview with Ticio Escobar the shaman said: 'When I cease to sing I fall ill. My dreams have nowhere to roam and they torment me. I am old and in pain. At the end of the day, what good has it been to deny who I am?'

So spoke the shaman in 1986. In 1614, the archbishop of Lima ordered the burning of every *quena* and all other musical instruments belonging to the Indians, forbidding any dance or song or ceremony on grounds of *preventing the devil from practising his deceits*. In 1625, the Royal Audience of Guatemala prohibited Indian dances, songs and ceremonies on pain of a hundred lashes, 'for all such are of a pact with the devil.'

To strip the Indians of their liberty and possessions, every symbol of identity was despoiled. Indians were forbidden to sing, dance and dream of their gods, although they themselves had been hymned and danced and dreamed of by gods in the far-off days of Creation. From the colonial days of monks and

imperial officials through to the contemporary North American missionary sects, Indians have been crucified in the name of Christ. Idolatrous pagans require saving from the flames of hell through evangelisation. The Christian God is invoked as an alibi for the pillage.

Archbishop Desmond Tutu talked of Africa in terms that apply equally to our Americas: 'They came. They had the Bible and we the land. They ordered us to close our eyes and pray. When we opened our eyes again, they had the land and we the Bible.'

In contrast, doctors of the modern state prefer the alibi of an illustration: ignorant savages require saving from the twilight by means of civilisation. Then as now, racism translates colonial plunder into an act of justice. Colonialism's victim is regarded as subhuman, with only an aptitude for superstition, not religion, for folklore not culture. A subhuman worth only subhuman treatment, whose scant value accords with the low price awarded the fruits of his labour. Racism legitimises colonial and neo-colonial plunder, through every century and on the various levels of successive humiliations, Latin America treats its Indians like the world powers treat Latin America.

Gabriel René-Moreno was the most prestigious Bolivian historian of the nineteenth century. One of the nation's universities is named after him. This product of national culture preached that, 'Indians are asses who procreate mules when crossed with the white race.' He had weighed an indigenous and a mestizo skull which, according to his scales, weighed between seven and ten ounces less than a white person's. Therefore he considered the former as *cellularly incapable of conceiving of the notion of republican liberty.*

The Peruvian Ricardo Palma, contemporary and colleague of Gabriel René-Moreno, wrote that, 'Indians belong to an abject and degenerate race.' And the Argentine Domingo Faustino Sarmiento praised the long liberation struggle of the Araucanian Indians by saying: 'They are the most indomitable, meaning the most stubborn of beasts, least adapted to the European process of civilisation and assimilation.'

The most vitriolic racism in Latin American history can be found in the world of its most famous and celebrated intellectuals at the turn of this century, and among the liberal founders of the modern state. Occasionally these men too were of Indian stock – like Porfirio Díaz, author of the capitalist modernisation of Mexico, who forbade Indians to walk down the main avenues and sit in the squares of the capital unless they exchanged their cotton breeches for European trousers and their sandals for shoes. Those were the days when the world market was determined by the British Empire and a *scientific* scorn for Indians afforded rulers a mantle of impunity as they robbed them of their land and labour.

The marketplace required – for example – coffee, and the coffee required more land and more labour. Thus – for example – a former president of Guatemala, the Liberal Justo Rufino Barrios, reintroduced the forced labour of the colonial era, bestowing Indian lands and peons upon his friends and allies.

Racism is demonstrated with blinding ferocity in countries like Guatemala where Indians persist in remaining a majority despite frequent waves of extermination.

Even today you can find no worse-paid workers. Maya Indians receive 65 cents for cutting a *quintal* of coffee or cotton, or a *tonelada* of cane. The Indians cannot even plant maize without permission from the armed forces, and cannot move around without a work permit. The military imposes widespread labour conscription to sow and harvest export crops. The plantations use pesticides fifty times more toxic than the maximum tolerable to humans; the women's breastmilk is the most contaminated of any in the western world. Take Rigoberta Menchú whose youngest brother, Felipe, and closest friend, María, died in childhood as a result of pesticides sprayed from crop-sprayers. Felipe died working in the coffee-fields, María in the cotton. The army then did away with the rest of Rigoberta's family and her community with machetes and bullets. Rigoberta alone survived to bear testimony.

Officialdom recognises with blithe impunity that 440 indigenous villages were erased from the map between 1981 and 1983, via a campaign of mass extermination that assassinated or disappeared many thousands of men and women. The highland 'clean-up', part of a scorched earth policy, also cost the lives of countless children. Guatemalan soldiers are confident that the vice of rebellion is genetically transmitted.

Until now the history of the Americas had not had its Indian version. On the eve of the Spanish conquest a Maya prophet, mouthpiece of the gods, proclaimed: 'When the codices are complete, the jaw and the hands and the feet will be untied.' And when the mouth is no longer gagged, what will it say? What will that *other* voice say, that voice that is never listened to?

According to the conquerors' viewpoint (until now the only one), Indian customs have always served to confirm either diabolical possession or biological inferiority. From the earliest stages of colonialism, Church and Crown have considered the Indians in terms of the following rhetoric:

Do the native Caribbean islanders commit suicide to avoid enslavement? Such acts do no more than demonstrate an innate idleness.

Do they go about naked, their bodies as bare as their faces? This but the shamelessness of savages.

Do they know nothing of private property, sharing all possessions and lacking the desire for riches? This shows them to be more closely related to apes than to men.

Do they bathe suspiciously often? By this they resemble heretics of the Muslim sect, who burn so brightly in the fires lit by the Inquisition.

Do they never strike their offspring but leave them to roam unhindered? Thus is revealed their inability to administer punishment or instil doctrine.

Do they believe in their dreams and follow their voices? This can only be either by Satan's influence or their own blind stupidity.

They eat when hungry rather than at stipulated hours? A clear indication of their inability to dominate their appetites.

They make love when they experience desire? Thus the devil induces them to revert to original sin.

Homosexuality is accepted? Virginity is endowed with no particular significance? So do they live in the antechamber of Hell.

In 1523, the Nicaraguan headman (*cacique*) asked the conquistadores: 'As for your king, who elected *him*?' The *cacique* had been elected by the elders of his community. Had the king of Castille been elected by the elders of his?

Pre-Columbian America was vast and diverse, rich in

democratic models that Europe failed to recognise and of which the world still remains ignorant. To reduce indigenous American reality to the despotism of Inca emperors or to the bloodthirsty practices of the Aztec dynasty is equivalent to reducing European Renaissance reality to the tyranny of its monarchs or the sinister rituals of the Inquisition.

According to Guaraní tradition, for example, *caciques* were elected by an assembly of men and women – and the assembly dismissed them if they failed to comply with the collective mandate. Among the Iroquoi, men and women governed on equal terms. The leaders were men but it was the women who appointed and removed them and who retained the power of decision, via a Council of Matrons, over most of the fundamental business affecting the entire community. At the turn of the seventeenth century, when Iroquoi men went to war on their own behalf, their women went on conjugal strike. When the men were obliged to sleep alone they soon shelved their plans to govern alone.

In 1919 a Panamian general in the San Blas islands proclaimed: 'The Kuna Indians will no longer wear their traditional dress (*mola*) but will clothe themselves in a civilised manner.' He further declared that henceforth the Indians would refrain from painting their noses but paint only their cheeks (as they should), and that they would never again wear gold nose-rings but only ear-rings, as they should.

Seventy years after this declaration, the Kuna Indians of today continue wearing shiny gold nose-rings and multicoloured *mola*, whose weave combines an astonishing sense of beauty and imagination: they wear their *mola* every day of their lives and into their graves when death receives them. . .

Through collective labour, ancient agricultural techniques rendered the mountainous deserts of the Andes fertile. In the hands of major private landowners producing cash-crops, modern technologies are converting the fertile Andean terrains – and many others – into an expanding desert.

To revert to 500-year-old techniques of production would be absurd. No more, absurd, however, than to disregard the catastrophes of a system that crushes humanity, rapes the land and poisons rivers to maximise profits. Is it not absurd to sacrifice people and nature on the altars of the international market? We live this absurdity, accepting it as if it were our only possible destiny.

The so-called primitive cultures remain dangerous for they are founded on common sense. A common sense that, through a process of natural extension, is also a community sense. If the air belongs to everyone why should the earth require an owner? If we came from the earth and will return to the earth, perhaps we too can be slain by the crimes committed against our earth? The earth is our cradle and our graves, mother and partner. We offer her the first draught and the first mouthful: we offer her rest, we protect her from erosion.

Our system spurns what it fails to understand, and fails to understand what it fears to know. Racism is but another mask for fear.

A black poet from inland Bahía recounts: 'First they robbed Africa of me. Then they robbed me of Africa.'

African memories have been mutilated by racism. We continue behaving as if we only had European forebears.

At the end of the last century, the English doctor John Down identified the syndrome which today bears his name. He believed that any chromosomal alteration implied the *regression to an inferior race* bound to generate *Mongol idiots, Negro idiots and Aztec idiots.*

At the same time the Italian doctor Cesare Lombroso

ascribed the physical characteristics of blacks and Indians to those he termed *born criminals*.

Such views accorded a 'scientific' basis to the suspicion that Indians and blacks are naturally inclined to criminality and mental debility. Indians and blacks, traditionally taken as instruments of labour were henceforth also to be regarded as 'objects of science'.

Around the same time as Lombroso and Down, the Brazilian doctor Raimundo Nina Rodrígues set himself to study the negro problem. Nina Rodrígues, himself a mulatto, reached the conclusion that 'mixing blood perpetuates the characteristics of the inferior races', thus 'the dissemination of the negro race in Brazil will forever remain a factor in the national inferiority of our people'. He classified Brazilian culture as a clinical case study: black religions were entered under pathology; trances were hysterical manifestations.

Soon afterwards an Argentine doctor, the socialist José Ingenieros, wrote of how 'the negroes, ignominious scourge of humanity, are closer to anthropoid apes than to civilised whites'. To demonstrate their irremediable inferiority, Ingenieros offered a final proof: 'Blacks have no concept of religion.'

In fact, *religious concepts* had crossed the ocean with the slaves in the traders' ships. One proof of the obduracy of human dignity: only the gods of love and war reached the shores of the Americas. By contrast, the gods of fertility, who had multiplied the harvests and slaves of the masters, tumbled into the waters.

The gods of the warriors and lovers who made the crossing were obliged to go in disguise. They had to dress up as white saints in order to survive and help the millions of men and women, violently abducted and sold out of Africa, to survive. Oggun, god of iron, succeeded in passing as Saint George or Anthony or Michael. Shango, for all his fire and thunder, was transformed into Saint Barbara. Obatala became Jesus Christ and Oshún, divinity of fresh waters, became the Candlemas Virgin.

Forbidden gods. In Spanish, Portuguese and other colonies including the British-run Caribbean, even *after* the abolition of slavery, it was still forbidden to play drums or blow African pipes. Even possessing the statue or picture of an African god carried a mandatory prison sentence.

A dark skin betrays inalterable structural defects. From this stems the most tremendous social as well as racial inequalities, citing laws of heredity by way of self-justification.

Humboldt observed as much two hundred years ago, and so it continues throughout the Americas. The pyramid of social class is dark at its base and white at the top. In Brazil, for example, racial democracy consists in keeping the whitest on top and the blackest beneath. James Baldwin wrote concerning blacks in the United States: 'When we left Mississippi and came north, we didn't find freedom. What we found were the worst positions in the workplace, and it's there we've remained.'

Asunción Ontiveros Yulquila, an Indian from northern Argentina, today evokes the trauma which scarred his childhood: 'Good and proper people were those who resembled Lord Jesus and the Virgin Mary. But father and mother didn't look anything like the statues of Jesus and Mary I saw in our church at Abra Pampa'.

One's face can be an error of nature, one's culture a proof of ignorance or a sin to be explained. To civilise is to correct.

Biological fatalism, stigma of the inferior races congenitally predestined to indolence and violence and destitution, not only prevents us from seeing the real causes of our historical misadventures. Racism additionally prevents us from knowing – or from acknowledging – certain fundamental values which despised cultures have miraculously succeeded in perpetuating and which still, for better or worse, find expression despite centuries of persecution, humiliation and degradation. Such fundamental values are not museum pieces. They are historical ingredients, indispensable to our invention of an America without either rulers or ruled. Such values *accuse* the system that denies them.

A short while ago, the Spanish priest Ignacio Ellacuría told me that the whole business of the Discovery of America seemed a ridiculous one. According to him, an oppressor is incapable of discovery: 'Rather it is the oppressed who discovers the oppressor.'

He believed the oppressor to be incapable even of self-discovery. The true reality of the oppressor can only be perceived by the oppressed.

Ignacio Ellacuría was riddled with bullets for having believed in an unpardonable capacity for revelation and for partaking of the risks of his faith in its powers of prophecy.

Was he assassinated by Salvadorean soldiers or by a system that could not confront the gaze that denounces them?

The old potter passes on his prize pot to the young potter. So the tradition gets handed down among North American Indians. An artist reaching retirement hands his favourite piece to the artist starting out. And the young potter doesn't retain the pot for purposes of contemplation and admiration but smashes it on the floor, recovers the fragments, then incorporates them in his own pottery.

The continuity and fertility of memory.

Future time as the repetition of past time? Does America have a splendid past ahead of her? Nothing of the kind. The memory of the vase to be modelled, the memory of a life to be lived. For navigators awaiting the wind, memory is a port of departure.

youth

columbus' children

JAN ROCHA

From the day the Spanish and Portuguese embarked for the Americas, they viewed the 'new world' as somewhere to loot and exploit rather than settle and develop. For five centuries Latin America and the Caribbean have provided Europe with cheap raw materials for its commercial and industrial wealth. Today these countries even provide babies for childless couples to adopt. Where once galleons were loaded with gold and silver to keep European monarchies afloat, today annual transfers of billions of dollars bolster western banks with grossly inflated debt repayments. Over the centuries sugar and coffee, copper and iron ore, rubber and timber, meat and beans have flowed from the region, while the massive human misery involved in their methods of production have afforded scant concern to the importing nations.

Within societies based on exploitation, children are seen merely as smaller, less efficient units of production rather than as future adult citizens who need to be educated, prepared and trained for a productive life. In contemporary Brazil, millions of children go to work rather than school. In Bolivia, small children spend their infancy on the pavements, behind their mothers' makeshift stalls. In Peru, adolescent boys work and die in the gold-mines of the Amazon.[1]

In the 1950s, Orlando Vilas Boas spent years exploring central Brazil, contacting Indian communities so they could go deeper into the forest, out of the way of advancing roads. He said he never saw Indians hit their children: childhood was a time to play and learn before the ritual passage to adulthood.

Five hundred years ago, the conquistadors introduced a system of *encomienda*. The theory was intended to be enlightened. 'A group of Indians is consigned by the king to a colonist and his dependents for two or three generations, that they should be protected and instructed in the Catholic faith.' In return, the worker paid the colonist the goods or labour otherwise demanded by the Crown. Forced to spend longer and longer periods gathering *yerba* tea in the jungle, thousands of Guarani Indians succumbed to diseases, many introduced by the colonists. According to a contemporary account, so 'an infernal circle begins, with the destiny of those who remain worsening as their numbers diminish. The wife is severed from the husband, the children from their parents. When they die, the Spanish bury them anywhere. They show more deference to their dogs and horses . . . and all this results from their insatiable thirst for gold and riches.'

With the mass extermination of the Indians, slave-traders

---

1. Maxime Haubert, *La vie quotidienne des indiens et des jésuites du Paraguay au temps des missions*, Paris, 1967

began to introduce African slaves within fifty years of the Conquest. Over forty million were transported in all, approximately half of whom died on the journey. When the traffic to Brazil was stopped in 1888, an estimated eight million had been unloaded at her major ports. The sociologist Gilberto Freyre described how, to maximise profits from the inhumanly-overcrowded slaveships, where space and supplies were calculated to the last degree, children and adolescents were often preferred over adults. In 1812, for example, one Bento José da Costa imported forty slaves, only two of whom were 'bearded negroes', the rest being, 'youngsters, youths and children'. Once landed they would soon develop into mature men and women who could be retailed at the highest prices.[2]

By contrast Freyre's research, based on newspaper advertisements of the time, shows repeated evidence of physical deformities which, he imagined, had been caused by the nightmarish conditions of their transportation. 'There developed among the slaves, in particular among the children and youngsters who suffered the horrors of those voyages, diseases and deformities which are reflected in the announcements regarding 'new slaves' who ran away during the early years: scurvy, bow legs, TB, rickets – because the generally unhygienic conditions of the slave ships were prolonged in the slave quarters on the plantations, where they lived under low roofs without benefit of sunlight.'

Harsh working conditions added to the toll of visible physical decline. One advertisement sought a runaway called 'Caetano, aged twelve, with a cross branded on his left arm and a bald patch in the middle of his head from carrying heavy volumes'. Fleeing adolescents were already clearly identifiable by the scars of punishment. Germano, aged seventeen or eighteen, ran away from the 'California' sugarmill in 1870 with a chain still around his neck and 'recent marks of punishment' on his buttocks. Not unsurprisingly, 'there is a permanently sad look on his face.' Sixteen-year-old Gregorio who fled with him had 'many signs of burns on his stomach as well as punishment marks on his buttocks'. The sugarmill owner warned: 'Should they be caught, they require watching with vigilance, as when previously recaptured they have attempted to commit suicide.'

2. Gilberto Freyre, *O Escravo nos Anuncios de jornais Brasileiros do Seculo XIX*, Companhia Editora Nacional, 1979

Cândida, an eighteen-year-old runaway, had a tin mask secured over her mouth with a padlock. Freyre explains that this was normal practice for those so hungry they would even eat earth – 'a common practice among our slaves.'

The advertisements studied cover both genders and all ages — including one in 1859 for a seven-year-old, in a lot with a horse suitable for a cabriolet. While Freyre himself was a great defender of the theory that Brazilian slavery was more benevolent than its North American or British counterparts, he also noted the numerous references to slaves who stammered, speculating that this resulted from 'the experiences of extreme fear and fright suffered by young children under the despotism of their severely authoritarian masters, which had terrorised and traumatised them for ever.'

Slave children were not only subject to fear and punishment but to early separation from their mothers. On 3 February 1859 the *Diario de Pernambuco* announced the sale of a 'negro woman aged twenty-five, [who] gave birth ten months ago, with milk, without the child. She cooks, makes sweets, irons and sews.' Another entry for the same day advertised a good cook 'with a child aged three, a very pretty thing suitable for spoiling: in case the buyer does not want the child, the slave can be sold alone.'

So it is that today's street children, who are predominantly black, come from a centuries-long tradition of families arbitrarily broken, whose members have been separated and traded as chattels. For every slave child adopted and raised as a member of the plantation owner's family, there were scores who were forced to undergo branding irons and whipping posts, excessive hours of labour, and the unhealthy living conditions and poor food of the *senzala*, the slave quarters.

Slavery in Brazil was abolished a scant hundred years ago, in 1888. It became untenable for a variety of reasons, including mass escapes and the army's growing refusal to pursue runaways. By the end of the last century new industries were starting up – and the cities were growing, at least partly as a result of government policies which encouraged 'white' immigration to prevent Brazil becoming a 'black nation'. Preference in awarding jobs was given to the European arrivals over the former slaves. A rootless and roving army of the latter were forced to choose between stealing and moving on or settling wherever unwanted land could be found, mainly on the hillsides and riverbanks around Recife, Salvador and Rio de Janeiro, or in roadside hamlets beside the plantations that afforded them seasonal employment. In the 1930s, Brazilian writer Jorge Amado described a group of homeless boys living in an abandoned warehouse beside the port of Salvador:

Then Legless looked long at the sleeping children. They numbered about fifty, without a mother, father or master between them. The only freedom they possessed was to run wild on the streets. They rarely had it easy in life, and obtained essential food and clothing by carrying bags, stealing wallets and hats, through holdups and occasional begging. Because a lot of the gang didn't sleep in the warehouse, there must have been over a hundred children altogether. They spread themselves through the doorways of tall buildings, on the docks, in overturned boats on the sands of the Porto da Lenha where the firewood came in. Not one of them complained. Sometimes one would die of an illness they couldn't treat. It was only when Father José Pedro dropped by at the right moment bearing God's love, or the maedesanto priestess Don'aninha, that the patient obtained some relief. Never that a child would have at home, Legless was thinking. And he found the joys of freedom slight when compared with the misfortunes of lives such as these.[3] *(Capitães de Arela/Captains of the Sands)*

---

3. Jorge Amado, *Captains of the Sands*, New York, 1988

Jorge Amado wrote fifty years ago, when the greatest danger the children had to face was capture at the hands of the police, or sometimes torture and removal to the Reformatory. Today's street children now face the added danger of elimination by so-called 'extermination gangs', police and ex-police who claim to be vigilantes bent on ridding society of potential bandits. Some hire themselves out to groups of traders who have been robbed, and many are already involved in crime as a way of life. Killing, even killing children and adolescents, becomes a habit to them and – more frightening still – to the public as a means of dealing with a problem increasingly perceived as one of public security untouched by government policies.

The national independent research organisation Instituto Brasilero de Análises Sociais e Econômicas (IBASE) explained in a recent study how the murder of minors is rationalised:

Minors, pickpockets, young muggers – in many instances the press, like society, does not hesitate to describe the victims in negative terms, criminalising them and purporting to find the motive for killing them in their implied guilt. In this way the deaths are absorbed, not as the murder of children and adolescents, but as the liquidation of another crook or street kid threatening public safety.[4]

IBASE found the majority of young victims had never been in trouble with the police, or had been to reformatory or had possessed firearms. Only 11 of the 457 under-18s killed in 1989 were carrying drugs and only 10 of these were allegedly involved in trafficking. IBASE concluded – 'We therefore consider this indiscriminate stigmatisation of working-class children and adolescents as criminals deserving of the death sentence as, to say the least, irresponsible.'

The children in Jorge Amado's book were orphans who ended up on the streets because they had no homes. Most of today's street children in theory have homes and only a few have lost both parents. Many have fled homes of extreme poverty and deprivation, have already been through foster-homes where they have suffered ill-treatment from their step-parents.

In the Rio *favela* of Parade de Lucas a woman called Iracema told of how her thirteen-year-old son, Luciano, who had taken to the streets, was killed. 'He was with two friends when a police car stopped and picked them up. The police accused them of attempting to break into a shop and took them to a lonely spot where one of the men played Russian roulette with his gun. It went off and the bullet hit Luciano. The police dumped his body outside a motel and drove off. They didn't attempt to get help or do anything to save his life.' The other two boys went into hiding, too scared to testify against the policeman. Iracema's youngest son was listening as she told her story. He was wearing his dead brother's T-shirt with the bullet hole through it.

In São Paolo Ellida dos Santos, a young woman who works for the Catholic Children's Pastoral, described how adolescents were persecuted by the police in the city centre:

'On the morning of the 5 January 1992 a group of boys was intercepted by some men in plain clothes, believed to be policemen. The boys were beaten up and one was hit by three bullets; one in the leg, one in the groin and one in the lung. He's now in hospital in a serious condition. His mates are in a state of panic because of daily beatings and death threats for being around the city centre. The aim of the police is to clean up the city streets and squares and prove that there aren't any more street children.'

One of the boys described his daily routine. 'I sleep together

4. *Lives at Risk* (*Vidas em Risco*), IBASE, 1991

with eight others in this corner here beside the church. We spend the whole day trying to find a way of getting some money so we can eat. Some of the policemen are just nasty and out for trouble. Others are okay, they talk to us. I want to get a job. If I go on stealing I'll end up in prison, now that I'm over eighteen. A lot of my mates have died on the streets, from Aids, an overdose or by being killed.'

Brazil's street children are the result of decades of government neglect of social services in pursuit of economic progress. This neglect was accentuated under the military regimes of 1964-85 when all opposition was stifled, criticism was silenced by censorship and social programmes were treated as communist propaganda. When the generals finally stepped down, their civilian successors acknowledged the social debt they inherited but failed to make any significant change to their priorities.

As public investment falls in schools, healthcare, welfare and housing, the Brazilian population is effectively bypassed by any kind of state infrastructure. As political and business corruption and mismanagement of funds is added to the impoverishment generated by continuing high inflation and recession, the weakest members of society are the worst hit. Within this sector, children are among the most vulnerable.

In 1991 the Brazilian Institute of Statistics (IBGE) published a survey of social indicators[5] which found that 63 percent of the country's 60 million children and adolescents live in families with a monthly income of less than half the minimum wage (between US $50-$80). The poorest half of the population saw their share of the national income drop from 13.4 percent to 10.4 percent between 1981 and 1989.

In addition, 60 percent of infants under one year old live in homes without basic sanitation – in the hillside shanty towns or in the waterside shacks on stilts or in mud-and-wattle countryside huts. Only 72 percent of children from low-income families attend school – because there is none nearby; because the basic equipment for attending is too expensive; or because their work is essential to the home or family income. Of every 100 children starting school, only 25 complete first grade. Nearly a fifth (18 percent) of youngsters aged 10-14 work full-time and most of those under 18 work over 40 hours a week and are unregistered, which renders them ineligible for sickness, accident, pension, or unemployment benefits.

I saw some of these child-labourers in Acailandia, a smoky town of sawmills and pig-iron smelters in the eastern Amazon. In a pit behind a sawmill two boys aged 12 and 13 told me they work 10 hours a day filling the pit with timber rejects to make charcoal. For each pitload, which took 2-3 days to burn, they earned approximately $4.00. The sawmill enjoys tax exemption and government subsidies for providing

5. *Children and Adolescents (Crianças e Adolescents)*, IBGE, 1991

'economic development to the region'. It is located within the Greater Carajas development project, which in turn receives European Community and World Bank loans.

Throughout Greater Carajas children are employed to make charcoal. This is then sold to the pig-iron smelters, who also rely on government funding but mainly export their product to Japan. A Brazilian reporter described the scene in one charcoal camp as follows:

> In the camps, everyone works. Even the children whose nomadic way of life prevents them from attending school. They suffer the most from the smoke and the heavy nature of the work. . . . Almost all suffer from respiratory problems . . . [and have] allergies and burn marks on their skins.[6]

Like his slave ancestors, 13-year-old Lourival de Oliveira carries the marks of his work on his body: There are 'burns on the soles of his feet, snake bites on his legs, his skin and hair are black with dust. He has been travelling for six years with his parents and five brothers and sisters on the charcoal trail that follows the forest clearances.'[7]

Lourival is conscious that his thin body and small size results from the heavy work at the furnaces: 'It's the charcoal that stops us growing.' The pittance earned from his sweated labour is deducted before it even reaches him and goes to pay the boss's bills. Under a system that has changed little since the days when slaves were denied any disposable income through debts to the 'company store', Lourival and his family always owe more than they can earn. The work-camps are so distant from the nearest shops that they are forced to buy food and essentials from their boss, and are kept permanently in debt for doing so.

In 1989 the four pig-iron smelters at Carajas consumed 1.2 million trees, causing ecological devastation. In neighbouring stretches of the Amazon, trees are being cut back and the water table reduced for another reason. Here poor families from surrounding provinces flood in to the *garimpo*, the gold mines. Hundreds of thousands of men, many still teenagers, grub for specks of gold in the rivers and mud flats. Despite the risks of malaria, landslides as the riverbanks collapse with the tunneling, and frequent violent deaths – and the minute chance of surviving all this to hit the jackpot – prospecting has an air of hope and independence denied those who work as *peãos* on cattle ranches, migrant harvest labourers or on city building sites.

Bars and brothels follow the men to their makeshift camps and lawless shanty-towns. Most of the girls working the brothels are in their teens or younger, and many are tricked into working there. A reporter from a São Paolo newspaper, aided by a Catholic priest and with the support of university researchers and a children's organisation, investigated the situation of under-age girl prostitutes.[8]

They discovered that they are held in bondage by brothel owners who claim they have incurred debts they know nothing of, and must work to pay them off. Once a girl is brought to town with promises of a 'good job' as a waitress or shop assistant, the brothel is rapidly substituted as her destination with debt as the mechanism of her enslavement. She is forcibly prevented from escaping until the 'debt' incurred for her transport in from the countryside, her lodging, food, clothes, and perfume is settled. One girl wrote of her experiences to the researchers: 'If we try and escape they go after us. If they catch one of us, they beat or even kill her.'

Many girls abandon any hope of a better life. Fifteen-year-old Luciana, sick with malaria, told the reporter: 'It's terrible here, but there's nowhere else to go to. I don't know how to read or write. I don't know anything. The only thing I can do is sell my body.'

6. Mehanne Albuquerque, *Ecologia e Desenvolvimento*, January 1992   7. Ibid.   8. Gilberto Dimenstein, *Folha de São Paolo*, February 1992

According to the Catholic priest Father Bruno Secci: 'When I began working with street children in 1973, there were few young girls among them. Now nine and ten-year-old girls commonly work as prostitutes.'

To maintain the supply of young girls to the Amazon brothels, recruiters comb the region. Some fathers sell their daughters in the hope that they will do better or earn more in the town than in the poverty of the countryside. Virgins brought to the city are auctioned to the highest bidder. The São Paolo newspaper found that the local police turn a blind eye in return for bribes from the brothel owners and concluded: 'The prostitution of younger and younger girls is one of the clearest symptoms of Brazil's social crisis.'

A further symptom affects a still younger age group: babies. What is particularly macabre is that it is frequently those most closely charged with their protection – lawyers, judges and social workers – who abet and even organise the sale and export of infants. Overseas childless couples are often willing to pay thousands of dollars for adoption papers that give them 'legal' access to bypass any rigorous conditions of adoption in their home countries. Since the social workers who procure the babies and the lawyers who arrange for their disposal abroad rarely meet the adoptive parents, few – if any – procedures to ensure their suitability are followed and the transaction is a purely commercial one that primarily benefits the intermediaries.

While some Brazilian mothers may surrender their babies fearing that *they* otherwise won't receive the care and education they need in growing up, a Parliamentary Committee of Enquiry concluded in 1991 that 'mothers who did not want to hand over their babies have been "induced" and put under psychological pressure to give up their children.'[9] The Committee proved that the lawyer most frequently accused of procuring babies for unlawful adoption was president of his local Bar Association's Council for Children and Adolescents.

The Ceára Committee of Enquiry report continues: 'To achieve this criminal intent, this organisation [representing also judges and social workers] turned the Juvenile Welfare Department into a veritable export bank for babies. Cases were manipulated, documents falsified, babies and identities swopped around, all with the intention of masking the commercial objective of these international adoptions.'

Until that time comes, the young people of the Kaiowá Indian people, survivors of the once-teeming Guaraní communities, will continue to commit suicide. In twelve months from 1990-91, twenty-nine youngsters aged thirteen to nineteen killed themselves by drinking pesticides or hanging themselves from trees with creepers. A further thirty-six attempted suicide and failed. For a young Kaiowá living on an overcrowded reserve close to a city, the only prospect of work is canecutting for a pittance on the plantations. Alcoholism is rife. Churches of all denominations have sprung up in the reserve, obliterating the traditions and customs that previously afforded young people continuity and hope for the future. Under such circumstances, suicide becomes a way out of an intolerable situation introduced by the invasion of their lands five hundred years ago – an invasion that is still continuing today.

In recent years, several thousand Brazilian babies have been adopted by foreign couples, mostly from Europe and especially from Italy. For Brazilian children, the future will only begin to improve when investment in development is seen to be investment in people.

9. Report of the CPI (Parliamentary Committee of Inquiry) set up by the Legislative Assembly of Ceára, August 1991

Snorting drugs with a knife, Santiago, Chile

Hand with a bottle of glue. Medellín, Colombia

Drug dealer smoking 'crack', Medellín, Colombia

Dawn for a homeless youth, Mexico City

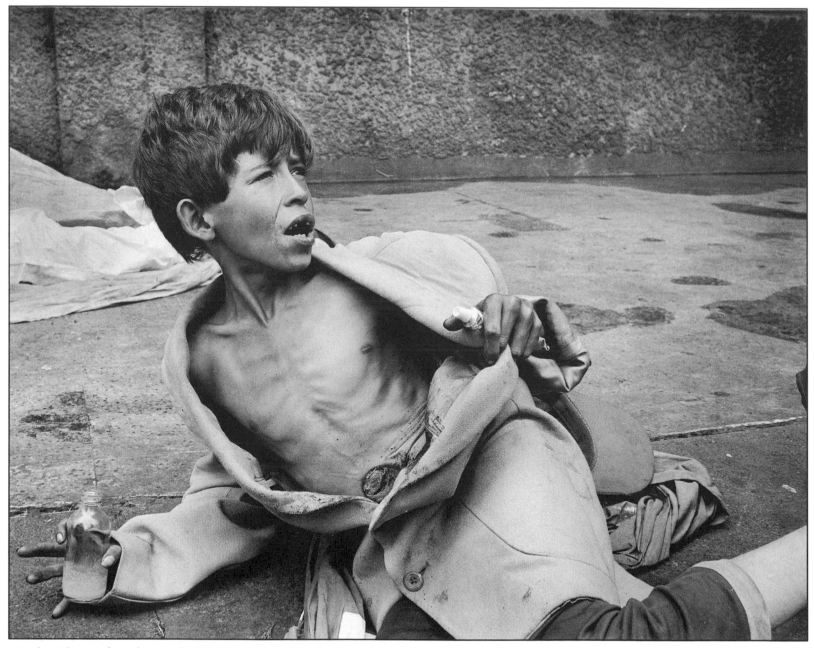

Youth with an infected wound in the streets of Medellín, Colombia

Behind bars at a rehabilitation centre, Bogotá, Colombia

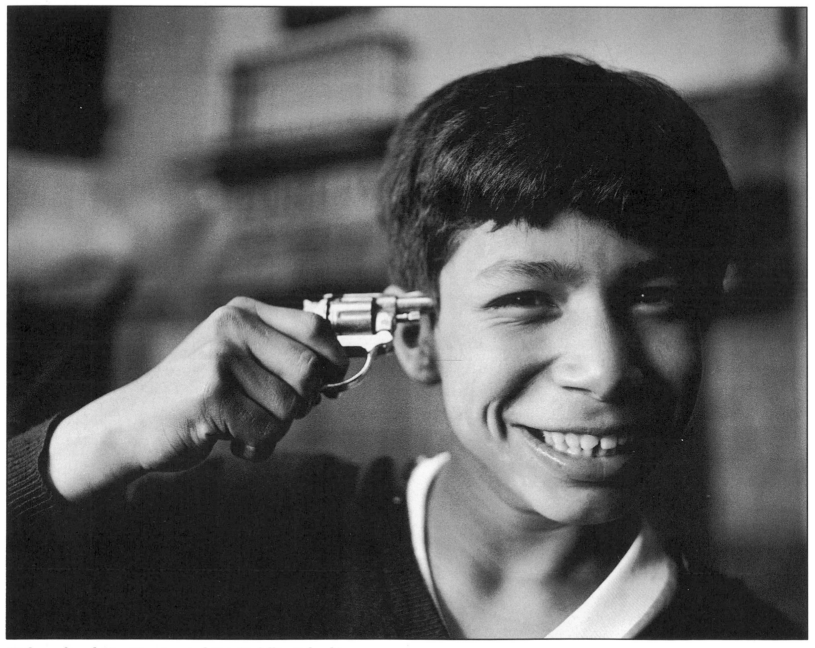

High on glue playing 'Russian roulette', Medellín, Colombia

Street circus at traffic lights, Mexico City

Playground in Havana, Cuba

Only a revolution is capable of totally changing the educational scene in a country, because it also totally changes the political scene, the economic scene, and the social scene. The levels of ignorance and illiteracy, the numbers of children not attending school are really frightening in the economically exploited nations. Why? Because in reality there is not the least interest in remedying these conditions.

Sleeping rough in Mexico City

A doorway in the old Colonial quarter, Santo Domingo

Red Cross worker comforting a suffering drug abuser, Bogotá, Colombia

Name: Beto

Age: 14

Occupation: Used to work crushing cardboard. Now sells sweets and fruit at traffic lights. Walks the streets, avoids the police and sniffs glue. Sleeps in the street.

Ambitions: Meet the TV compère Silvio Santos. Buy his mother a house at 'Porta da Esperanca' [Gate of Hope].

Heroes: I don't really have any . . . I don't know anyone that good.

Virtues: Protects the girls in his group.

Faults: Sniffs glue.

Successes: Silence – no reply.

Mistakes: I didn't want to turn out like this.

Would like to meet: TV stars in the street. Anyone.

Would like to avoid: The police.

Favourite films: *Rambo* and *Cobra*.

Favourite book: Primary-school exercise book.

Favourite food: Anything.

Hobbies: Watching Mutant Ninja Turtles on television sets in shop windows.

Philosophy of life: Share with friends. Hit or run away from enemies, depending on their size.

Religion: I wanted to be a Catholic, but a Catholic who goes to work. There's no way I would want to be part of one of those evangelical churches.

Favourite city: Well it has to be the one I'm living in, don't you think?

Sleeping rough in Medellín, Colombia

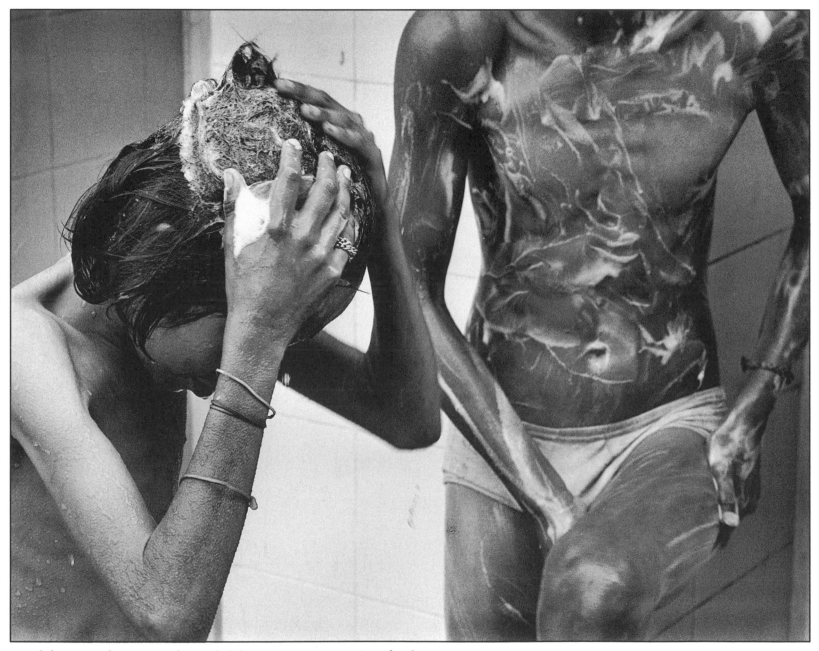

Youth having a shower at a drug rehabilitation centre, Bogotá, Colombia

We sniff glue because we need to. We steal – watches, necklaces. We don't have anywhere to sleep, we don't have anywhere to stay – that's why we steal. I steal. I steal, I walk around, I sniff glue, and then I can't do anything. I haven't got a Dad – he died seven years ago. I have eight brothers and sisters and I can't really stay at home, so I live on the street. That's how I lead my life.

Addict with bottle of glue, Medellín, Colombia

Poem from Father Aristide

I am here to cry out to and to remind you that:

We have come from far away in order to arrive at a remote destination. We have left the ravine of death in order to arrive at the top of the mountain of life.

Are we there yet?

No.

Do we want to get there?

Yes.

Can we get there?

Yes.

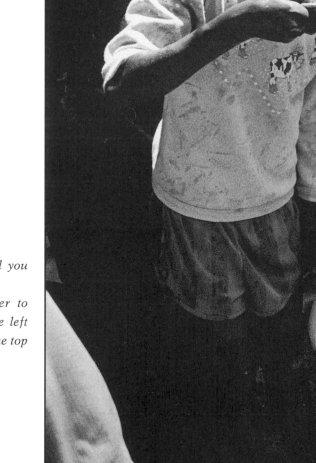

Playing with water at 'Lafami Senlavie' orphanage, where Father Aristide used to work, Port au Prince, Haiti

Quechua children playing in Pimbaro, Chimborazo, Ecuador

The original people are very different in their living habits to the newly-arrived colonisers. They were already used to the climate, the insects and the woodland animals. So two distinct ways of life emerged in parallel with little in common. The *Collas*, as they call us, didn't speak Spanish at all well. In fact, some of us could scarcely speak it at all – least of all the women for we all talk Quechua or Aymara amongst ourselves. This makes the *Cambas* feel superior, for although they are mainly illiterate and keep to their own dialects, they also speak good Spanish. Whenever there was a discussion or an argument, they'd say: 'You *Collas*, maize-guzzlers, go eat boiled potato! Learn to wear sandals!' As *Collas* we then had to stand up for ourselves, telling them: '*Cambas* go eat boiled plantain! Eat monkeys you barefoot *Cambas*, since it was they who went without shoes.'

power cycles

the white wall and the spiders

DANIEL MOYANO

(*From an interview with Andrew Graham-Yooll*)

In Buenos Aires once, asked by someone on the paper *La Opinión*, I tried writing about my detention but never got beyond the second page. Perhaps this is my chance to tell the story in full.

Before the military takeover of 24 March 1976, I had received threats from the Triple-A, a paramilitary death squad. At the time, our local radio station was reading over the air a chapter a day of my novel *The Devil's Trill*, which had been published the year before. The station itself received threats to the effect that if they kept reading my book their building would be blown up. When I was threatened as well, I went to the then Governor of the Province of La Rioja, Carlos Menem, who is standing as the Peronist candidate in the presidential elections, and he gave my home police protection.

On the day of the coup, I was 260 miles away in Córdoba, trying to enrol in the philosophy department of the university. There was gunfire, which I had to go out of my way to avoid as I headed for the bus terminal. I returned home to the city of La Rioja that night. As we entered town, I saw that control posts had been set up as if the place was under occupation. A girl getting off the bus was fondled by a soldier, giving us a foretaste of the abuse that was to come. We were all made to lie down on the ground and we were threatened. But the girl was being touched up while the soldier cooed sweet words to her.

When I got home, I learned that the military forces had picked up almost all of La Rioja's intellectuals. Many of them worked on the newspaper *El Independiente*; one, the poet Ramón Eloy López, was a well-known Christian Democrat. Of the three members of the Rioja Communist Party, who were a father and two sons named Leonardi, one was taken into custody. A few members of the Peronist Youth were arrested too, as well as the architect who'd built the local jail and who was placed in one of its four isolation cells.

I told my family not to be surprised if I too were arrested. I got up the next morning to begin studying for my university entrance; I was in my pyjamas, sitting at my desk, which faced the street, reading Charles Bally's *Language and Life*, published by Losada in 1944.

I had just opened the book (which I have kept as a sort of relic), when I saw a car stop outside. It wasn't an army car, but three soldiers got out of it dressed in fatigues and carrying sub-machine-guns. A fourth soldier stayed in the car. The three began slowly to make their way towards my house. My daughter, María Inés, who was three at the time, was fast asleep, and my fourteen-year-old son Ricardo was up playing with two friends. My wife Irma was off in some other part of the house. I hurried to open the door before the soldiers kicked it in or even before they knocked. When I did, they asked, 'Daniel Moyano? You are to come with us.' And they barged in. That was on 25 March, the day after the coup. Obviously my name was on some list.

I asked if I could get dressed. They said I could but must hurry and they accompanied me to the bedroom. I put on a pair of trousers, shoes, a shirt, and, since I didn't know how long I'd be, a light jacket. That's the time of year autumn begins in Argentina. I wanted to take my house key but they told me not to. I asked if I should take my identity papers and they said that wouldn't be necessary. This gave me a moment of fright. In Argentina, even to go out to the corner, it is advisable to carry your identity card.

At the time, in addition to my work as a novelist and musician, I was a correspondent for the Buenos Aires daily, *Clarín*. In that capacity, I had always exposed any failings on the part of the government of La Rioja – within the limits of what a right-wing newspaper like *Clarín* allowed. But my concern was not so much with the government as it was with calling attention to the problems that beset the province, one of the poorest in the country.

I was driven in silence to the army barracks, which was quite near my home in Corrientes Street. There, pushing and shoving me, they marched me to an enormous room where half the intellectuals of La Rioja were standing up against the wall with mattresses beside them. But they were not allowed to sit down. I saw Carlos Mamonde, my assistant on *Clarín*, and any number of friends and acquaintances.

We were there from eight o'clock in the morning until around six in the afternoon. At midday we were brought a revolting gruel of the kind served up in police stations. No one even attempted to eat it.

They made us fill in a card on which we had to give our names, professions, and ideologies. I didn't know what to say for ideology, because I had never established exactly what my ideology was. My upbringing was not Catholic but Protestant. I could have put down Christian, but I was not sure a religion implied an ideology. I suppose what they wanted me to put down was Communist. Leonardi, one of the three Communists in La Rioja, later told us that, as a good party member, he had written the word Communist in capital letters. But I was not a Communist; nor could I write down capitalist. I was a writer. I don't know what piece of nonsense I put down in the end.

At six that afternoon we were herded together and made to board a huge bus. There were about fifty of us. We had been held in silence all day except for the guards' words of command. Nor had we been allowed to sit. I have no idea what the mattresses were there for.

The bus's windows were covered with newspaper, either so we couldn't see out or so nobody could see us. But through the windscreen I could see where we were headed. Behind us, as the back windows were also uncovered, we could make out a lorry with thirty soldiers in it pointing sub-machine-guns at the bus.

The man beside me, who came from the town of Chilecito some way off over the mountains, asked me where we were being taken. 'From here to the city arch is three blocks,' I told him, 'and it's two blocks to the turnoff towards the La Rioja jail. If in two streets we turn left, that's where we're going; if we pass it, then we are leaving the province.' The latter, we later learned, would have proved even more dangerous.

That moment, when it seemed that the bus ought to be turning left but wasn't, felt like an eternity. But finally it did. We arrived at the jail in the dark. I was familiar with it because whenever something at home needed mending we took it to the inmates there so they could earn some money. Half of La Rioja did the same.

We were shoved against a wall, and then the guards began to shout at us. There were quite a few soldiers in addition to provincial police and the border patrol from Chilecito. Facing the white wall, we were made to stand a pace apart. 'Stare at the little spider on the wall and at nothing else,' we were ordered. 'If there is no spider, find one. Don't look at anyone else and don't speak. Our guns are very jealous and they might let out a shot or two.' The part about the little spiders I put into my novel *The Flight of the Tiger*.

There was a sound of safety catches being released and then a terrible silence. Carlitos Mamonde, who was beside me, said, 'I think they're going to kill us.' My mind was in a daze. I had no way of understanding what was going on. I was in a state of stupor. I was wondering how they were going to clean the wall afterwards, it was so white.

As we waited to be shot in a silence that lasted for who knew how long, we suddenly heard our thirty guards break out into a forced laugh. It had all been a sham. Then one of them put a spoon behind our backs under each of our belts. I shall never figure out why. When he finished this, another man came along and took them away. Again the guards all burst into laughter. They probably knew we were hungry and would think that the spoon meant they were going to feed us. But they didn't. Was it some form of torture? I don't know.

Next, one by one, they asked our names and professions. I said journalist. 'What paper?' I was asked by a fat man with three chins. I told him *Clarín*. 'So you're the slave of Noble's widow, then.' I didn't answer, but it was obvious that they were out to be offensive. They took away my shoelaces and belt, and, holding up my trousers, I was shoved along with the butt of a rifle. We climbed a staircase, a door was opened, and with a kick in the behind I was forced inside. They locked the

door, and no light filtered in from anywhere. I never knew whether it was day or night. I was in that cell for eight days, fed through a little opening six inches square. I found a nail on the floor and, once I got used to the dark, I scratched on the wall the lines of the musical staff. I wrote notes and sang them. I also recalled these verses from the *Romancero*:

I did not know the night from day
but for a bird that sang each dawn:
an archer slew it; God make him pay!

After eight days a man came and led me to another cell, this time not an isolation cell. It had a small window, from which I could look down into both the front and rear courtyards. From time to time I could see other prisoners standing in front of the glass doors of their cells. All day we could not sit or lie down but had to stand up against the glass doors so the guards could see us. I would take advantage and do some exercises whenever the guard turned his back. When they brought our meal – the revolting prison meal – it was so bad we used it as an excuse for not eating. Nor did I want to ask for water, because that would mean having to urinate, and sometimes they wouldn't let you go.

The prisoners kept leaving their cells to be interrogated. They interrogated Ramón Eloy López, the Riojan poet and teacher, a close friend of mine, who was in the next cell. When we went to wash our plates, we would pass each other. We couldn't speak but we managed to mime words and make signs. I asked how he'd been treated. 'They didn't torture me,' he told me that night. 'They asked about my friends, and I said you were one.' At that point the guard shouted for silence. I asked him for the time and he said, 'You are incommunicado.'

I began to measure time by the shadows and sunlight and by a little bird which appeared, as in the *Romancero*, every day at the same time, landing on the same roof tile (this I also recorded in *The Flight of the Tiger*), and flying off in the same direction. In that cell at least I saw daylight. Father Pelanda, the army chaplain, came and told me I should have faith in God and resign myself. Then an officer came in and asked how I was. Not at all well, I told him. Another officer appeared. He was not, like all the other jailers and soldiers, from Buenos Aires. He was from La Rioja, which surprised me. I saw he had the face of a Riojan, and so I wasn't afraid; I did not associate this crime with Riojans. He began shoving me backwards, prodding me in the chest into a corner of the cell, where I fell down. Looking towards the door, since evidently he was not supposed to talk to me, he said, 'Listen, Professor, I want to tell you that your family is well. Is there anything you need?' It turned out that he was a relative of one of my students at the Conservatory. I asked for a toothbrush and a book or two.

Books were impossible, but he said he'd try. What book? Something acceptable, say the *Arabian Nights*, he suggested. Much later, the writer and poet Mario Paoletti, who remained in that jail until 1980, told me that he had seen one of the common jailbirds in the courtyard downstairs reading my novel *El Oscuro*, which had won the Primera Plana Prize in 1966. It seemed very odd to me that they had let such a book in. My novel had been taken from La Rioja bookshops and burnt. They had burnt the copies at the army barracks, together with books by Julio Cortázar and Pablo Neruda, by which they did me an honour.

The next day an officer of the border patrol from Chilecito came to see me. 'Are you Moyano? I want to tell you something. You don't know me but I know you. I don't know what's going to happen to you. But whatever does, I want you to know that I am not a criminal. I am a soldier, but not a criminal.' I thanked him. In one way what he said scared me – his uncertainty. On the other hand, it was a human gesture.

The *Arabian Nights* reached me, and a toothbrush and a towel. It was April and the cold began. We had inflatable mattresses but mine had a puncture. I'd spend half the night blowing it up and the other half watching it deflate. The bed was a hard metal grille all I had to sleep on was that deflated length of canvas. Whenever I could I did exercises. I lost over fifteen pounds in eleven days.

I kept thinking that a helicopter was going to come and rescue us. Another prisoner later told me that he thought of making himself a great pair of wings out of glued matchsticks and cloth from shirts and flying away. But I thought about a celestial helicopter.

One day I spied out of my little window that Carlos Mamonde was being taken away, with his hands tied behind his back, by a subaltern with a sub-machine-gun. They were taking him to some sheds to be interrogated. I had seen a number of men pass that same way. When Carlos went by I saw that he tried to escape and that they fired a shot and that his hands were cut. I began to shake all over. At meal time I told someone, 'They've cut Carlos Mamonde's hands.' The next day I met Carlos and I stared at his hands. They were both fine. I asked if he had been tortured. 'No,' he said, 'they asked me about you.'

I had never before had hallucinations nor have I ever had them since. It appalled me. I have never been able to write about this, nor can I account for it.

Two days later, on my twelfth day of incarceration, the border guard from Chilecito reappeared at about eight o'clock in the morning. 'Please, don't say anything to anyone in your secret language. You're leaving tonight – free. I'm telling you so you won't be scared.' No one was ever told when he was moved if he was going free or going to be shot. That night, when they called, 'Moyano, outside with all your belongings,' the other prisoners looked at each other in fear. I managed to say to Mario Paoletti, 'I'm getting out. Is there anything you want?'

'The second volume of Dostoyevsky's works,' Mario said.

Once outside, we were put in a car. The wife of the poet Ariel Ferraro was there. She had been detained in another wing. Ramón Eloy López had been freed with us, and one other person. Only four were set free. In the prison the next day the beatings began.

We were taken to a delegation of the Federal Police. I was given back my belt and shoelaces, and we were each made to sign a blank page in a book. At the same time, we were told that we could not leave La Rioja. Someone in command, who was from Buenos Aires, said, 'You people must watch your step from now on; any false move might prove fatal.'

We went out into the street. I was four blocks from home. Nena Lanzilloto, Ferraro's wife, lived farther away. She was hysterical. I told her to come to my house and I'd drive her home. 'I don't want cars or houses,' she screamed. I left her and continued on my way. People appeared. The dentist Nato Pavani came out to greet me, quite surprised to see me. The names of those in custody were never made public, but word had got round.

When I reached home, my wife was crossing the street in our car on her way to see the military governor. She tried to see Colonel José Malagamba, who under Alfonsín has been promoted to general. It was he who had interrogated us and it is he who was responsible for the deaths or disappearance of sixteen Riojans. (My wife had also tried to see Pérez Bataglia, a colonel who was later taken to hospital with a nervous breakdown.) The next day, Malagamba would not see me, so I just waited for him outside his office. 'What do you want?' he shouted at me. I wanted to know why I had been detained. He said he didn't know. I wanted to know if I could leave La Rioja. 'Go anywhere you like,' he told me. 'As far as we in this military region are concerned there is nothing to stop you.'

My detention had been ordered by the regional commandant, General Benjamín Menéndez, uncle of the Menéndez who surrendered the Falkland Islands, and son of a thousand bitches. While we were in prison, he went to the barracks — I was later told this by a soldier – where he called together all our jailers, and, frothing at the mouth, screamed at them, 'I don't want prisoners, I want dead men.'

When I was told I could leave the province, I went straight to Buenos Aires, applied for a passport, returned to La Rioja, and in one week my wife and I packed up the house and we all went to Buenos Aires to wait for a ship. We sailed on the *Cristoforo Colombo*, of the Italian 'C' Line, on 24 May 1976, and on 8 June we disembarked in Barcelona. That was where I began a new life in exile.

Postscript: I had always believed we were transferred from the army barracks to the jail by bus and that, once there, I dreamed that we'd been transported in the back of a lorry and that an officer had pressed me down with his boot against my neck. For a long time I told others about this dream, then, years later, I met other survivors who had been with me on that night, and they tell me that what I dreamed was the business of the bus, that we had actually been transferred in the lorry and that they had seen how the officer had me flattened under his boot. (November 1988)

(From *After the Despots, Latin American Views and Interviews*, Bloomsbury, London, 1991)

Mural in Port au Prince, Haiti

Right wing political rally in Lima, Peru, 1990

Relatives of victims of repression in Santiago, Chile, 1985

President Balaguer, Dominican Republic

The Messiah

'The president arrives by helicopter and listens to the complaints of smallholders and landless *campesinos* who spontaneously and passionately air their grievances. When they have finished speaking into the microphone, they draw nearer to tell him their troubles, almost whispering into his ear as if in confession. They tell him about the overdue mortgage, the money they need for an operation, a sewing machine for the wife, a bicycle for a son, or a pregnant pig.

'Balaguer grants their wishes with an immediate order or makes sure that they are given a pass to see him in the presidential palace in Santo Domingo. Then he begins to speak, publicly ridiculing his own ministers and administrators for their incompetence or berating some local landowner for monopolising the irrigation scheme and leaving no water for the smallholders, "with the complicity of the military" – who, standing by, listen impassively to the president's attack. The *campesinos* worship him like some sort of messiah. A women in the audience in the village of Las Guáranas suddenly falls into epileptic convulsions.'

'No' to Pinochet poster, Chile, 1988

Prayer in the National Stadium

Forgive me for telling of my pain
  again and again.
Forgive these funeral processions,
this cell, this jail, this anguish
  that enter my poems.
Forgive me, friends, this repetition.

What has happened is that since then
  all I can do is remember.

I beseech you, St. Quixote,
to visit me this night,
in this fearful night of dread
to comfort me in my delirium.
Give me the strength to bear
this long night and those ahead,
yet longer and yet darker,
Nights in their cruel hands.

Today at the grey dawn,
St. Sancho come,
give us bread,
a sure and true tenderness,
in my veins.
The one necessity
for ever and ever
Amen.

Demonstrators holding hands outside Volta Redonda steelworks, Brazil

The last change of guard under military rule, Brasilia, Brazil, January 1985

A few weeks ago I stopped by at the home of an old friend, a Mexican born of 'pure Aztec blood'. We made use of the occasion, having not met up for a while, to go out and consume quantities of tacos washed down with much tequila.

. . . Between one gulp and the next and without overstepping the mark of good behaviour, he adopted a serious tone in which to inform me: 'If those bastard gringos would only get out of waging wars around the world and came along with us to eat tacos, how good life would be!' 'Fine,' I answered, 'but what has any of this to do with you?' 'It so happens that one of those gringos is my son.'

. . . My words of protest arrived late on the trails of others' protests. But I couldn't resist the temptation to contribute my grain of sand to the general struggle, at least in defence of tacos and the good things of life.

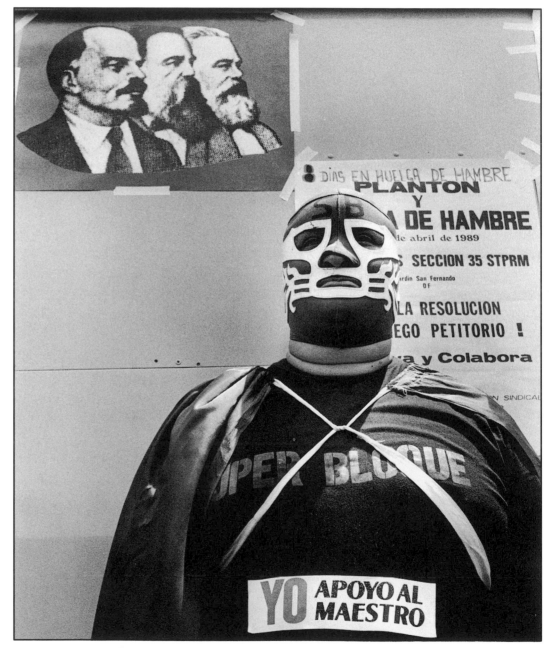

'Super Barrio', a shanty town Robin Hood, Mexico City

President Cristiani and vice-President Merino during election rally in El Salvador, 1989

Archbishop Rivera y Damas celebrating mass (after the murder of six Jesuit priests, their housekeeper and daughter), El Salvador, 1989

Bishops and cardinals waiting for the Pope, Argentina, 1987

Daniel Ortega with poster of Sandino, Nicaragua

A little frowning man in a big hat, he (Sandino) had become a collection of stories. . . it was Sandino's hat, and not his face, that had become the most potent icon in Nicaragua. A hatless Sandino would not be instantly recognisable; but the hat no longer needed his presence beneath it to be evocative. In many instances, FSLN graffiti were followed by a schematic drawing of the celebrated headgear, a drawing that looked exactly like an infinity sign with a conical volcano rising out of it. Infinity and eruptions: the illegitimate boy from Niquinohomo was now a cluster of metaphors.

President Violeta Chamorro, Nicaragua

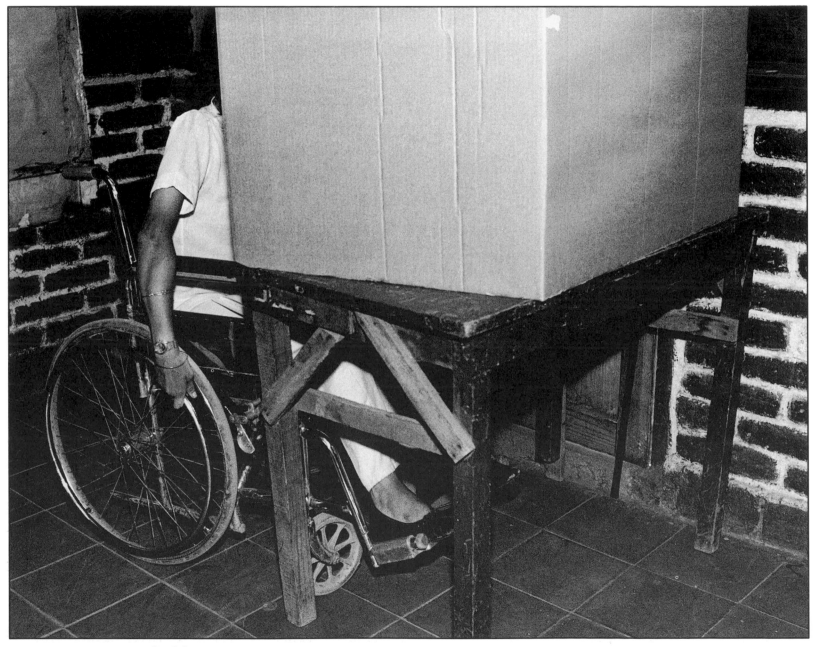

War victim voting in a wheelchair, Nicaragua, 1990

Opposition leader Seregni greeted by supporters after his release from ten years in prison under the dictators, Uruguay, 1984

Election campaign, Peru, 1990

Fidel Castro and Gorbachev, Havana, Cuba, 1989

migration

expulsion, exile and return

RIGOBERTA MENCHÚ

I don't see myself as particularly different to the majority of Guatemalans forced to flee from our homes. The repression is what has driven all of us out, causing the displacement of over a million people (out of a population of approximately eight million). There are not only those who, like myself, fled abroad after many death threats and the murder of most of their family but also 'internal refugees', those who have fled to other parts of our big country where they cannot maintain their traditional ways of life. These people can be found in the shanty towns and rubbish tips of major cities; working illegally, in conditions of slavery, on the vast plantations of the south coast; or in the Communities of Resistance, groups of people who, hounded by the army, have taken to the hills. Since many flee from village massacres carried out by the army, the Communities are bands of people who may not even speak each other's languages to begin with but who learn to travel and live together.

You have only to look at our national reality ever since the CIA toppled Arbenz (a liberal, democratically-elected president, whose demise was followed by 32 years of junta rule) in 1954, to understand the reasons for leaving. Guatemala is a country of 60,000 widows, 43,000 'disappeared' – it's where that term was first used for military kidnaps and death squad

executions – and 30,000 people forced to live wild in the mountains. My country is a silenced country and the voices raised abroad on our behalf have never consistently accused the true violators of human rights, the armed forces.

People have been even more loath to denounce those guilty of 'impunity', the arrogance with which the military break existing laws with violence. If you come to Guatemala, the atmosphere of terror generated by military impunity is undeniable, yet no one is ever punished and the crimes continue in the most brazen way. So you can see the reasons for our exile: the loss of our relatives and loved ones, the destruction of our homes, and families broken by torture and killings. Sometimes I think the miracle is that any of us got out alive at all!

At other times I am aware that in Guatemala you always walk with death. When I made my first attempt to return, on 18 April 1988, after seven years' exile, it was incredible how I was treated. It made such an impression that I still have nightmares about it. Four of us from the political opposition, the United Representatives of the Guatemalan Opposition (RUOG), had negotiated our return, together with sixteen foreign observers. It had been made very clear, through the United Nations Human Rights Commission, that we were there to contribute to the national dialogue then taking place.

We had also been through a whole process of diplomatic mediation via Guatemalan embassies in Geneva, New York, Washington and Mexico. There appeared to be a consensus that our visit would generate a new democratic opening, and there was a lot of support for this.

But at the airport we were greeted by four hundred National Police, who abducted two of us as we descended from the aircraft, before we'd even entered national territory. They seized us at midday and we spent an hour and a half under lock and key at the airport. We were kept in a detention room, though no one else was allowed to know this. To us it seemed like centuries as we convinced ourselves — based on how well we knew our National Police – we'd never again see our friends and companions. I can't really explain what it means to live through something like that, with no guarantee that one would come out of it alive. And we were terrified of night falling, knowing that that would lead to another century, a century of waiting and blackness. Eventually, we were released at eight-thirty in the evening.

While we were effectively held prisoners – they even removed our passports – others attempted to contact their embassies but were forcibly prevented. However they did manage to draw our disappearance to the attention of the journalists who'd come to interview us on our return. It came out over the radio and in the afternoon papers, which I'm sure helped to obtain our release.

They never told us who'd given the order for our illegal detention or allowed our lawyer to see us. I'm recounting all this as an example of how the law functions in Guatemala: there are no constitutional guarantees and no international laws that apply. We were apparently released as a 'special case', not because we'd been properly interrogated and defended under the terms of the law, but because there were 5,000 Guatemalans demonstrating at the airport.

The atmosphere for our whole stay was determined by our arrival. The climate of intimidation and the sense that our lives were at risk accompanied us everywhere, making our work very difficult. That type of pressure made us decide to leave, but five of us returned on a new United Nations delegation the following year, in 1989. There were no obvious problems to begin with, but within a few weeks, the death threats began. Some were relayed by telephone via the popular movement (peasant, trade union and women's organisations). That also put other people's lives at risk. In Guatemala, matters are so contorted that death threats appear almost as a gift of life: the great majority of those subjected to 'extra-judicial executions' don't have the benefit of a warning. As a rule victims aren't informed that they are going to be kidnapped! We were a special case and in a single day we received nine death threats.

Those of us in the RUOG had all previously been threatened and, in two cases, captured. After the murder of so many politicians, trade union leaders and other organisers in the popular movement, all opposition voices seemed to be silenced. That was why we formed the RUOG in exile, and how we came to work on human rights for the United Nations in Geneva. (Molina, who came with us and who'd also been kidnapped and tortured by the military, is our current representative there.) This work still continues since the situation in Guatemala has in no way changed, far less improved. Guatemala is a country devoid of democracy.

In the event, I flew out of Guatemala City in 1989 a few minutes inside the deadline set by the death threats. I'd been given 72 hours to leave and when I did, paper bombs were released in the capital denouncing me for fleeing for my life and leaving others at risk behind. Other leaflets rejoiced that for the first time I was fleeing death and had abandoned the country.

At eleven o'clock that same night my remaining colleagues were warned that there was a car bomb activated under the building in which they were staying. The whole place had to be evacuated in a matter of seconds, the timing was so short. The RUOG representatives were strenuously 'encouraged' to leave the country. The situation had been made intolerable for them.

I spent a month in the country in October 1991, but that has nothing whatever to do with any improvement in the situation there, just that a new context was created by all the events surrounding the 500 Years of Resistance campaign. There was a huge gathering for a five-day conference in Quetzaltenango, bringing together indigenous people from throughout the continent, many of them very high-profile, which always helps in ensuring personal security. There were also others of considerable international weight attending as observers, such as Mme Mitterrand.

On the other hand, if I simply wanted to return tomorrow, to be in my home country, I'd have to harbour a desire for martyrdom. Or rather I could always decide to go, but would I be able to leave?

The advantage of living in Mexico is that I really don't feel as if I'm in exile. My work is on the steering committee of the Peasant Unity Movement (CUC). Through the organisation I'm fully involved in the 500 Years of Resistance campaign: I find it far more exhausting to do this sort of work touring abroad, but when I get back to Mexico the whole dynamic changes and I settle into working creatively, solving problems and determining new initiatives appropriate to our organisation – and in passing it on so that others may learn more of what we do.

I work with a Guatemalan co-director, in charge of the work orientation and production of the CUC. Work that involves all sorts of other organisms: diplomacy, the United Nations, fraternal indigenous groups throughout the continent and in solidarity with our fellow Guatemalans – without forgetting the 45,000 in the refugee camps of southern Mexico, whose experience of exile is so entirely different from my own. Or the 200,000 in the United States, 99 percent of whom work as illegal immigrants because their claims to obtain status are always turned down.

In any case, what so many of us really want is to return home, to our remaining families, to our land and to our country. For me there would need to be profound changes before I could go back and lead a normal life as a politician in the region. When a civilian government was finally elected in 1986, President Cerezo invited me to return, and even suggested my taking up a political appointment. But I've always replied that I shouldn't need permission or protection from anyone to return home – not from the army, nor any government functionary. And of course, the moment I went back for the first time in 1988, it must have seemed like a gift to them since – obviously – I was not there to live or even to stay for long, there were so many restrictions on the part we could play depending on the precise political moment at which we arrived.

In terms of international relations, however, our arrival suited the government down to the ground: we were being used as a banner to proclaim: 'See, everybody, democracy has returned to Guatemala' meaning that we – and people like us – were now safe to return to the country. But of course we had to be aware of the political risks we were taking, aware of the fear that death could come at any moment, so of course it was a momentous experience. What persists as the most significant sensation of all, however, is that of conviction, of knowing that despite all the risks it was more important to go back.

So the issue of return takes on a grander dimension: the personal aspect can be one of fear; the political point is to raise a profile. The moment when I was detained at the airport was one of self-discovery, when the joy of going home became an act of faith, of my saying to myself: 'Well, Rigoberta, now you know why you returned.' And I think our return did bear fruit, since until then our work was never even mentioned at any kind of national level, there was a total news blackout even on the work undertaken by the United Nations. And for us it was a first opportunity to interweave the work we had been doing internationally with what needed doing nationally.

It was also an opportunity for me to introduce my book, *I, Rigoberta Menchú*, into its country of origin. It had previously circulated only in clandestine form, although the San Carlos campus of the national university was supposed to own one copy, from which so many photocopies had been taken that it was in tatters. Even so, a reason given for my detention was precisely to do with my book which they imagined reflected writings by Marx or Lenin, which in fact I hadn't read. The other reasons they then came up with were my (genuine) participation in peasant struggles and my supposed headquarters in Nicaragua and Cuba, from where I meant to indoctrinate my compatriots, travelling illegally between the countries.

The two key elements were, however, the book and the film that was made from the book called *Cuando las Montañas tiemblan* [When the Mountains Tremble]. Those, along with various other bits and pieces I'd written, apparently constituted a crime of defamation against the state and, although there is no official censorship, the book remained banned. Even today in Guatemala it's a risk to keep a copy in your house – yet abroad it's been translated into twelve languages and sold hundreds of thousands of copies.

Well, that, as I told you before, was my first experience of returning. For the tens of thousands of other refugees in Mexico, return is an absolute necessity. It goes against the grain for us, as a people, to see our children grow up in a foreign country. The children themselves feel neither Guatemalan nor Mexican, since their parents inculcate in them the love of a homeland they cannot even visualise. I recognise that this is a problem for refugees everywhere and at all times, that of making one's country real to the next generation. It has to be a constant source of pain to every mother and father to see their children grow up without a true and rooted sense of their own identity.

Conversely, just because you put down roots on whatever patch of land you find yourself in, you have to straddle the new as well as the old culture. Yet you take your traditions home with you when you return, and I think that young people must have great possibilities in going back to Guatemala, where their roots and their people belong, and their memory awaits them, as well as the very complex present conditions. Repressive institutions control our daily lives and the impunity with which the armed forces conduct themselves means that murderers walk the streets who can never be legally accused, still less prosecuted. So impunity is a point of departure not only for violence but also for a chain of injustices and impositions on people's daily lives, even in the most remote corners of the country. The armed forces have invaded some of the smallest and poorest villages, stealing and burning the land title deeds of self-sufficient farmers and *campesinos*. They also force the illiterate into 'signing' away their few possessions in total ignorance, in the presence of corrupt mayors.

The key to a safe return and to a change in existing conditions on the land when people do get back lies in organisation. There is a government department with the responsibility to assist with the return programme, but who would put their faith in programmes emanating from such a government? Our own experience has taught us that the only institutions we can trust are those we establish ourselves, just as we did with CONAVIGUA (the organisation of indigenous widows, whose husbands were killed by the army), with CONDEG (the organisation of the displaced), and with CUC (the Peasant Unity Movement). Here we need to take our cue from the Salvadoreans, who have created their own organisations in a fully democratic manner. For them, leaving their country has not signified abandoning political activity. Instead they have integrated their sense of identity with their political awareness and return home with them both reinforced. Hopefully, too, they take back with them a newly democratic way of life that has a part to play in the future of their country.

All this also connects to our 500 Years of Resistance campaign. The campaign is born of a longing, a desire in Latin America to revise its own history and include the indigenous people, with a new understanding not only of our economy and politics, but also of our identity and culture. This leads directly to a vision of the future that covers a much wider field than any single historical event. It has a large part to play in overcoming the present cultural fragmentation, which others choose to divide along racial lines.

Mestizaje (mixed blood) is, however, an accentuated reality

in all our countries and yet political manifestations are different in every case. Ecuador, for example, has never suffered any kind of internal armed conflict whereas Colombia has undergone the experience of *la violencia*, in the 1940s, and still has an armed revolutionary movement, now entering parliamentary politics. We have to sow the seeds of allegiance around common aims in order to forge unity out of both our common historical origins and our differing present-day situations.

There's a legacy of the Cold War that is still being imposed upon us, as Latin Americans, which still seeks to locate us as politically on the Left or Right, even on the Centre-Left or Centre-Right. This is used to undermine unity among distinct peoples, both within and outside Latin America. Which is why our campaign for unity constitutes such a beautiful vision. It goes against the current of dominant political thought, and has many obstacles to overcome before becoming a reality.

In the face of this it's bound to be something we, in every case, have to do for ourselves. To bring it back to our national level: in Guatemala we, the indigenous Maya, belong to twenty-two distinct language groups, yet it's clear to all that where the Ministry of Development is also the Ministry responsible for Military Counter-Insurgency we cannot put them in charge of our destiny. It's by starting from an analysis like this, then calling on all the international organisms willing to assist us (and here I believe the Catholic Church, of which I'm a member, has a major part to play) that the popular movement can engage in the struggle, the same struggle that is part of the 500 Years of Resistance campaign. At our last conference, which I attended in Guatemala last year, the Campaign included the phrase 'indigenous, black and popular' before the final word, 'Resistance'. This shows the groundsoil of our solidarity and how much we have yet to achieve on our own behalf.

Salvadorean woman watching as the air force bombards her refugee camp, El Salvador, 1989

Miskitos returning from refugee camps in Honduras to their homeland in Nicaragua, Cocos River, 1988

Yanomani family, sick with malaria, being airlifted to hospital Roraima, Amazon, Brazil

Refugee from the war in the Honduran border having a bath in a dirty pool, Managua, Nicaragua

Water polluted with mercury to extract gold at a clearing made by prospectors, Roraima, Amazon, Brazil

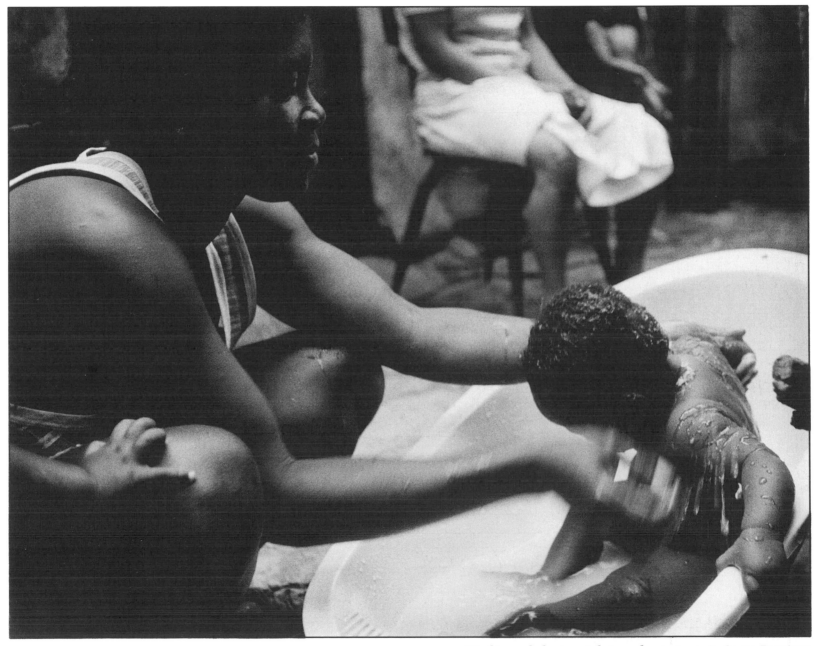

Washing a baby in a tub in a shanty town in Santo Domingo

Yanomani woman and child being airlifted out of their homeland, Amazon, Brazil

A long time ago, the sky fell onto the earth. A great shaman had died and his helper spirits, when they lost their chief, became so angry that they began to cut the sky with supernatural weapons, tearing it apart. The sky came loose and fell to earth, forcing the forest and the mountains down into the underworld, 'theeee!' People scattered in fear, 'aaaaa!' The sun and the night spirits also fell. This was due to Oman, who later created another sun and another moon. This earth on which we all live does not extend beyond the first sky, for which a fresh substitute appeared. Above this sky is the new celestial level where the spirit Mrooribe lives. Because the sky fell, the first ancestors were tumbled into the underworld where they became Aobataribe, cannibals with long teeth. Yet some people escaped from the underworld and stayed where we are now.

Refugees from the violence in the countryside settle in the desert in the outskirts of Lima, Peru

Miskito woman mourning her son killed by the 'Contras', Atlantic Coast, Nicaragua, 1988

Burning and clearing a patch of rainforest, Amazon, Brazil

Refugees at the football stadium in San Salvador

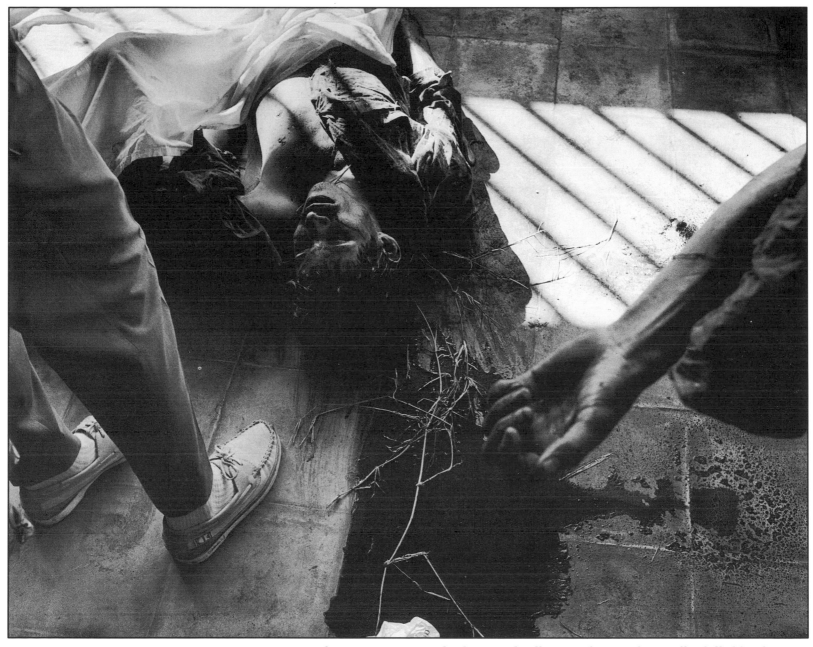

At the morgue in San Salvador. Nearly all are civilians and guerrillas killed by the army

Colonial quarter in Santo Domingo, Dominican Republic. Residents displaced for official Columbus celebrations

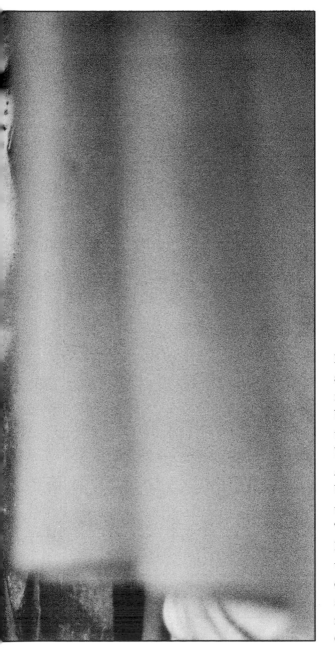

Poverty has no religion. If I, as a Christian, accept my brothers who practise our popular religion (voodoo) and love them as fellow brothers and sisters, then we can all live together in harmony. Remember, we don't have to *approve* their beliefs, just love them. And politics? Well people in this country, both Christians and Voodooists, have stood up against oppression all down the years. That is what politics mean, everyday politics. Remember that many of those oppressors were so-called Christians and voodooists engaged in political practice, but repressively. So it always comes back to attitudes, moral ethics and above all – don't forget I'm a Christian! – love.

Natives of San Juan, southern Ecuador on their way to take over unused farmland

Those who went to the mines worshipped the mountains over the mines, as well as the mines themselves. They called the mines *Coya*, imploring them for their metal. In order to achieve this they drank and danced in reverence of these mountains. Similarly they worshipped the metals, which they called *Mama*, and the stones containing those metals which they called *Corpas*, kissing them and performing other ceremonies.

Latin immigrants teaching lambada at a community centre in Islington, London

When I look sadly out from these strange/
  foreign lands
to the distant southern horizon,
I clearly sense the River Olimar flowing
and the scent of mountains on the breeze.

This sky is not the sky of my home,
this moon doesn't shine as mine did,
As the moon over my homeland
higher even than the shimmering stars
shone to light my highest hopes.

So many beloved looks, beloved voices,
missing from the bars and cafés where
  we met.
Others wander disconsolate through
  the world —
Ay! my homeland, how my heart weeps
  for you!

Chilean exiles dancing cueca at a community centre in London

Quechua women working communal land, Ecuador

Queueing for a visa outside the US embassy, Santo Domingo

Liking the opportunities and luxuries of America, Alberto Piñon started to think about leaving Cuba and settling in Florida. Alberto worked at the club six nights a week. It was a huge dance joint, festooned with papier-mâché pineapples, bananas and orchids. Its doors and windows were painted with silhouettes of bending palms. There was a long horseshoe bar and a huge bandstand where the orchestra played under a barrage of coloured spotlights. . . Famous people went into that place. One night the actor Errol Flynn showed up with an entourage of hangers-on. Showpeople, local politicians, gangsters and couples from all over the city out for elegant ballroom dancing came to the Royal Palms. There were women in tight dresses with skirts slit up to their thighs and net stockings held up by flowery garters. Their breasts flowed over their dress tops and wobbled when they danced. Big asses swayed during the rumbas and as *comparsa* lines circled the floor. The women wore as much perfume as Persian princesses, and the men tended to get out of hand, drinking too much and bumping into the walls.

Cuban exiles in Miami, USA

Racist graffiti, London

Métro users in a hurry, echoing footsteps. African drums, starving scrapers of violins. Beggars sitting on the floor, with the pathetic story of their lives written in chalk and a modest tin can for the paltry coin of charitable souls. Self-absorbed, implácable, blind faces of the horde of pedestrians coming toward you, as though out to settle accounts with the equally fierce one advancing with you along the white-tiled corridor, with its girls-using-natural-protein-shampoo, its Tunisian-Balearic hotels, its aperitifs, Italian pasta, cheeses, frozen foods. Fear of tripping, falling, being immediately trampled underfoot by the indifferent mob, hearing the roar of the trains, turning off down a side corridor, climbing flights of stairs, reaching landings, pushing doors open, arriving at last at an exit.

Arab in Belleville, Paris

informal economy

chanel in la chacarita

ISABEL HILTON

Alsinia showed me her house. It was in the La Chacarita district of Asunción, a warren of a shantytown that clings to the river bank. The streets are largely unpaved, the children barefoot in rubbish strewn alleyways. Some houses are built on land where the owners know that eviction is unlikely and it is worth building in brick. Others are made of the flotsam discarded by the affluent sections of society: cardboard, plywood, a bit of corrugated iron for the roof, if you are lucky. There was electricity, illegally connected to the city supply, water for washing from a street tap and water for drinking sold off a truck that passed daily.

Alsinia's house was better than average, as she pointed out and represented progress in her material life. For one thing, she had managed to occupy a site that was above the river's high water mark, so that she would no longer risk disaster in the annual floods. The safer site meant that it was worth investing in construction: her house had a solid foundation and a corrugated iron roof. Inside were two wooden cupboards that she could lock with a padlock. There were two rooms, one where she slept with the two older children and the other for the three little ones. There was no man in residence, for the time being.

Alsinia is a tiny woman in her early forties. She left school when she was nine, one of six children in a peasant family, and drifted to the city in her teens to work as a domestic servant. She lost her job when she became pregnant with her first child and now she sells herbal remedies in Mercado 4, Asunción's teeming central market, centre of petty commerce, contraband, crime and prostitution. Alsinia works there six days a week, from 5.30 in the morning to 8.30 at night.

In all of Alsinia's life, the state has done nothing for her, beyond four years of primary education that left her barely literate. Nor has she done anything for the state, beyond the acceptance that the burden of her existence, and that of her children, is something she must shoulder alone. She has never paid taxes; she has never registered to vote; she has never recorded either of her two marriages; she will never receive any social security or draw a pension. She and the state coexist, each indifferent to the other.

In Latin America, there are millions like Alsinia, people who live like Alsinia, in the informal sector. Parts of the informal sector are visible on the streets of any Latin American town, in the street vendors, the foodsellers, the shoeshine boys. For many years, the informal economy and the people in it were treated with suspicion in official descriptions of society or the economy: the informal economy was seen as the focus of petty crime, parasitical on the state by choice but tolerated because the state was incapable of offering an alternative means of survival. It was thought of as a problem that could be resolved through development.

In recent years, however, attitudes to the informal sector have been changing, as research suggests not only that the scale of the informal sector is much larger than was supposed and that, far from being parasitical on an official entrepreneurial sector, the informal sector is a locus of entrepreneurship that could, if understood and encouraged, make a dramatic contribution to economic growth.

One of the first descriptions of the scale of the informal economy was the result of research conducted by the Peruvian economist Hernando de Soto, of the Institute for Liberty and Democracy (ILD) in Lima. In *The Other Path*, a controversial book that became a bestseller in Latin America, de Soto reversed the conventional analysis of the relationship between the informal economy and the official sector.

It was the state, he argued, that constituted the problem because it supported a maze of laws and bureaucratic regulation that made legal entry into the economy all but impossible. Sheltering in this maze was a formal business sector that, far from representing entrepreneurial values, was engaged in negotiating its own protection with the state. The informal sector was both a creative response to the state's incapacity to provide for the basic needs of large numbers of its citizens and a potential reservoir of growth.

To illustrate the cost of legality, the ILD set up a fictitious two-machine clothing factory and attempted to register it legally. It took a total of 289 days of full-time work by the team of four university students and one administrative lawyer to deal with the red tape required. Bribes were demanded on ten occasions and paid twice, in order to proceed. The cost – US $1,231 – represented at the time 32 months of the minimum wage. No authentic small-scale entrepreneur, they concluded, could hope to operate legally.

Despite the difficulties created for them by the state, the informal sector, de Soto discovered, was responsible for well over half the nation's economic activity and, in some sectors, for nearly all of it. In Lima, Peru, 8 percent of the city's markets were built by black marketeers and 95 percent of public transport was owned and operated informally. Over half the city's housing was built by the informal sector which, between 1960 and 1984, spent 47 times the amount that the state spent on housing.

The battle for housing has produced one of the most intricate and complex sectors of the informal economy. Shanty towns may look haphazard, but they conceal high levels of social organisation and a set of hierarchies and power structures generated by the communities themselves.

The settlement of Bocanegra, in the district of San Martín de Porres, to the north of Lima, for instance, is home to 30,000 people. The land is desert, an expanse of dust crammed with huts that are built of woven reed mats nailed to wooden stakes. Entire families and their possessions are crammed into the dark interiors, cooking, eating, sleeping and washing inside a few square metres of space. There are no paved roads, no running water, no sewage pipes and, where there is electricity, it is available because of illegal connections to a nearby cable.

Bocanegra looks like misery. But to the inhabitants it is a victory, a toehold of security won through direct action against an indifferent state. Bocanegra is a squatter settlement, seized by 'invasion', that is going through the slow process of legitimation.

It is one of the absurdities of the situation that there is no good reason why invasion should be necessary: Lima is surrounded by empty land, most of it desert belonging to the state. In theory, a group of householders could negotiate the purchase of a block of land and build their houses there. But the nightmare of Peruvian bureaucracy renders such straightforward solutions impossible: there are 207 administrative steps involved in the purchase of a plot of state land. It can take four to five years to make the purchase and a further two to three years to obtain permission to build on it. For the large numbers of people who have migrated to the cities over the past 50 years, illegal occupation is the only way to house their families.

Invasions are carefully planned events that can involve several hundred families. Those who participate are expected to share the risks and the costs of the occupation and, in return, expect a fair allocation of the land seized. The occupations tend to take place at night, or in the early morning, often on national or religious holidays, in the hope that this will delay the police sufficiently for the squatters to establish themselves on the land. Hundreds of families have to be found transport; sufficient food has to be brought to keep them going for the first few days and the tasks of childcare, communal cooking, defence and the rapid erection of the first shelters assigned.

Bocanegra's success was in fighting off the government's attempts to dislodge the squatters and establishing a basis on which negotiations could open for the recognition of the settlement.

The Bocanegra invasion was planned for the day in 1985 on which Alan García took over the presidency of Peru. He had come to power on a populist platform that promised social justice and the date of the occupation was heavy with symbolic value. But three months later, the police tried to dislodge the squatters in an assault so violent that the nation was shocked. Squatters resisted with stones, but were eventually overwhelmed by repeated cavalry charges and tear-gas attacks. Their shacks were torn apart and burned as television cameras recorded the desperation of near destitute families trying to save their possessions from the flames.

Embarrassed by the publicity, the government reversed its eviction order and allowed the squatters to return to Bocanegra. The government also promised funds to survey the land and carry out the assignment of plots between the families, the first step towards the legal recognition of title, without which no electricity or water services can be supplied.

Three years after the government's recognition of the settlement, no survey had been carried out. The squatters again took direct action and contracted a private company to conduct the survey. It took just three weeks to complete. The squatters presented the government with the survey and began to negotiate for its official recognition.

Once the survey was done, a miraculous order began to appear in the chaos of the settlement. Lots were pegged out and the shacks reassembled in lines. Outside some of them, little fences were erected to shelter a few carefully tended plants. With the allocation of plots a slow and costly process of consolidation begins: the painful accumulation of building materials that will eventually transform a settlement of wattle and mud into a solid suburb of brick houses.

In communities less well-organised than Bocanegra, that transformation cannot take place. Beyond Bocanegra are small squatter settlements that will never make it. Some creep up mountain slopes that could, at any moment, become landslides. Others perch on ridges so steep and dangerous that people and houses regularly slide off. The people in these settlements are in a precarious limbo: they will not be dislodged by force because nobody wants the land. But nor will they ever win official recognition of their settlements or legal title to their plots. Without title, they cannot sell, sub-let

or mortgage their houses. Their efforts enable them to have a roof, of sorts, over their heads, but not to enjoy the financial value of what they build.

Invasion is a tactic most visible in the physical occupation of land. In Paraguay, since the fall of Stroessner, there have been hundreds of invasions of agricultural or forest land by landless peasants or families who had left the land in the 1970s to work in the construction boom that surrounded the building of Paraguay's hydro-electric dams. Once the projects were completed, many found themselves both jobless and landless and were forced into the informal sector to survive. When the dictator fell, they seized their opportunity.

The land invasions provoked bitter battles. The squatters were accused of targeting land that was already under cultivation and within easy access of roads. The squatters accused the Institute of Rural Welfare, a government agency charged with land reform, with offering them alternative land

that was not sustainable. If no agreement could be reached in the negotiations between the landowner, the Institute for Rural Welfare and the peasant groups, the squatters became liable for eviction. At the same time it was discovered that the Institute for Rural Welfare had massively abused its land reform function by handing out land to cronies of Stroessner.

Invasion also occurs, though less visibly, in the informal commercial sector. There it is a means of establishing a place in the market – either tangibly, in the form of a physical location from which to sell goods, or intangibly as, for instance, in the case of a transport route. Invasion is often followed by a process of negotiation with the authorities to legitimise the de facto operation.

To operate successfully in the informal sector demands a degree of organisation that is only slowly being recognised. Informal transport operators, for instance, frequently develop complex cooperative structures that provide their members with mutual insurance funds, undertake banking, regulate internal disputes, organise the wholesale purchase of materials and permit drivers who have no vehicle to have the use of vehicles belonging to other members.

In the informal housing sector, parallel power structures are developed to substitute for a state apparatus that does not function. They operate on democratic lines, with an elected leadership answerable to the participants and which regulates the occupation and negotiates with the formal sector on the squatters' behalf.

The struggle of the informal sector is a struggle first to survive, then to grow. Many of those who work in the informal sector are recent arrivals from the countryside. Some are refugees from inhospitable regions that offer little hope of education, health care or even relief from hunger. Some have lost the battle for land to big landowners or agroindustries; others are victims of natural disasters; still others of a concentration of land holding that does not allow a growing population access to what it needs for subsistence. They come to the cities, where they survive as they can.

The informal operators suffer from the deficiencies of the state in diverse ways. The state effectively prevents them from legalising their economic activity and because of their illegal status they run a number of risks: they cannot integrate themselves or their workforce into the social security system, should one exist; they find it impossible to obtain credit from the formal financial institutions and must rely either on family networks or on the informal financial sector – loan sharks who operate with punitive interest rates; they have no security of contract and cannot settle disputes through the law; they find it difficult to expand their activities and they have no formal defence against harassment by the state.

Little attention has conventionally been paid to these problems because the informal sector suffered from low status. It was seen as socially marginal and of little economic importance. Slowly, however, it is being recognised that the informal sector has much to offer the national economy. As Dr Martin Burt, a Paraguayan economist, pointed out: 'It takes $15,000 of investment in the formal sector to create 350 jobs. And Paraguay needs 45,000 new jobs a year. It can't be done the conventional way, but if you can help the people in the informal sector to expand, they will create new jobs with minimal investment.'

Dr Burt runs an institute in Asunción that specialises in providing financial support and advice to local micro entrepreneurs. Like Hernando de Soto, he believes that the informal sector represents the most dynamic sector of the economy and that if it can be encouraged to grow, it will stimulate the national economy to an impressive degree.

The assistance that Burt's institute offers is both financial and technical: he offers loans, at commercial interest rates, and provides courses in literacy and accounting. To qualify for a loan, a borrower must agree to take a course, for which he, or she, must also pay. She must also find partners for her loan who will guarantee repayment. Default, said Mr Burt, is very rare.

Alsinia, the seller of traditional herbs in Asunción's Mercado 4, is one of his clients. She has had eight loans over two years, of sums not exceeding US$35.00. Such loans would be insignificant in the formal sector, but they gave Alsinia a small working capital with which she was able to double her stock and therefore her turnover. Before she had access to this kind of credit, her only source of finance was from the market's loan sharks.

If Alsinia represents the bottom rung of the ladder, Narcissa Galeano, who is thirty-five, is counted one of the project's successes. She started in business by herself, turning out ties on a single sewing machine. Now she employs five young women. Her first loan from the institute was $850.00. She managed to repay it in eight months. Since then she has had nine consecutive loans and a perfect payment record. Her ties all carry a label that reads, 'Chanel Paris.'

Narcissa was very pleased with the label. 'We've started to sell directly to Argentine tourists in Encarnación. They are very keen on labels. We used to put Givenchy on them, but someone in Paraguay held the licence for Givenchy and he objected.' Nobody has the licence for Chanel. Her ties cost her 2,500 *guaranies* to make and she sells to wholesalers for 6,000. Selling direct to the tourists, she can charge 25,000.

Narcissa's workshop has crossed the frontier of legitimacy, in some ways at least. She holds a licence for the workshop and pays taxes. She does not, however, pay the legal minimum wage of $180.00 a month. In paying less than the minimum wage she is technically breaking the law, but the minimum wage legislation is one of Paraguay's least honoured statutes. Narcissa argues that it is prohibitively high and claims that all her workers earn more than they did in their previous employment. Her workers agree. Without Narcissa, said one of the cutters, she would have had little alternative but to continue to work in the supermarket where she had started at the age of twelve and where she was paid a derisory wage for a twelve-hour working day.

Narcissa's progress from informal businesswoman to legal workshop owner is a tribute to the tenacity and energy of informal operators who manage, despite government indifference or hostility, to support their families and to provide essential services to their communities. All over Latin America, the men and women who live and work in the informal sector present a reproach to the archaic and corrupt government structures that have marginalised them. Where formal legal systems have failed them, they have devised their own, informal systems. Where formal commercial and industrial structures have denied them entry, they have developed parallel operations. Where exhausted and discredited bureaucracies have tried to suffocate them, they have responded with flexibility and creativity.

Women vendors, Haiti

Flea market, Santiago, Chile

When the blue-white people came,
this is what they did to us:
They taught us to know fear.
They came to blight our flowers
so their own plant might flourish.
They wounded and despoiled
each one of our flowers.

Once upon a time our world was good
Then upon a time our gods were cast down.

They had held our wisdom,
and there was no such thing as sin.

Then the blue-white people came —
they castrated our Sun!

They burnt the face of our Sun.
It fell, shattering into fragments
upon the gods of today.

Do not forget us,
do not erase us from memory,
do not lose us,
look first to your own homeland,
look first to your own homes,
seed and root yourselves there!
Multiply and set forth
and come again
to the place from whence we came.

Aymara women trading in the streets of La Paz, Bolivia

'Tap-tap' in the streets of Port au Prince, Haiti

Fire-eater in Mexico City

My name is Juan Diego and I'm sixteen now but I left Tijuana when I was eleven because my parents couldn't afford to look after me any more. When I first came here a man made me work for him as a prostitute but I hated it – I kept getting infections. Then some workers from the Hogar Providencia started teaching us about personal hygiene, giving condoms to the boys in my *banda*. But the police always steal the condoms so I decided to take up fire-eating – for the sake of my health. So now my lips are chapped, my throat is raw and my lungs ache from the paraffin. It seems that if you don't want to die of hunger you have to live with diseases!

The priest came in from his inner room swinging a censer, the censer which he swung in our faces was a trussed cock – the small stupid eyes peered into my eyes and the banner of St. Lucy swayed after it. When he had completed the circle of the *tonelle* the *houngan* put the head of the cock in his mouth and crunched it cleanly off; the wings continued to flap while the head lay on the dirt-floor like part of a broken toy. Then he bent down and squeezed the neck like a tube of tooth-paste and added the rusty colour of blood to the ash-grey patterns on the floor. When I looked to see how the delicate Philipot was accepting the religion of his people, I saw he was no longer there. I would have gone too, but I was tied to Joseph and Joseph was tied to the ceremony in the hut.

Cock fighting in Haiti

Fishermen and empty baskets, Guayaquil, Ecuador

Musician sleeping, Quito, Ecuador

To be sure, at times there had been droughts and a famine that lasted two years, but all this was lost in time which held no dawn for Rosendo but only the pale stars of memory. The priest, Father Gervasio Mestas, officiated at the festival and he knew how to pray to St. Isidore in proper fashion. And the friars who came through the village would bless the flocks so they would multiply and grow thick wool. But one had to be careful not to be taken in by false friars. Because once two men dressed like friars passed through Rumi as they travelled about the hill country asking alms for their convent in Cajamarca. The lay brothers who accompanied them were driving along a herd of sheep and cows donated by ranchers, farmers and villagers. They blessed the herds of the givers with great solemnity, using words nobody understood and making the sign of the cross. And it happened that while they were in the district of Sartín, driving a herd so big it was like a roundup, a university scholar who really did know Latin and theology chanced to pass that way. He spoke to them, and the make-believe friars stood there, rooted to the ground, confounded by his questioning and knowledge. That wasn't the end of the matter, though. The people rose up in anger, and the imposters had to strip off their clumsy robes and run as fast as their legs could carry them.

Selling squeegees in the streets of Lima, Peru

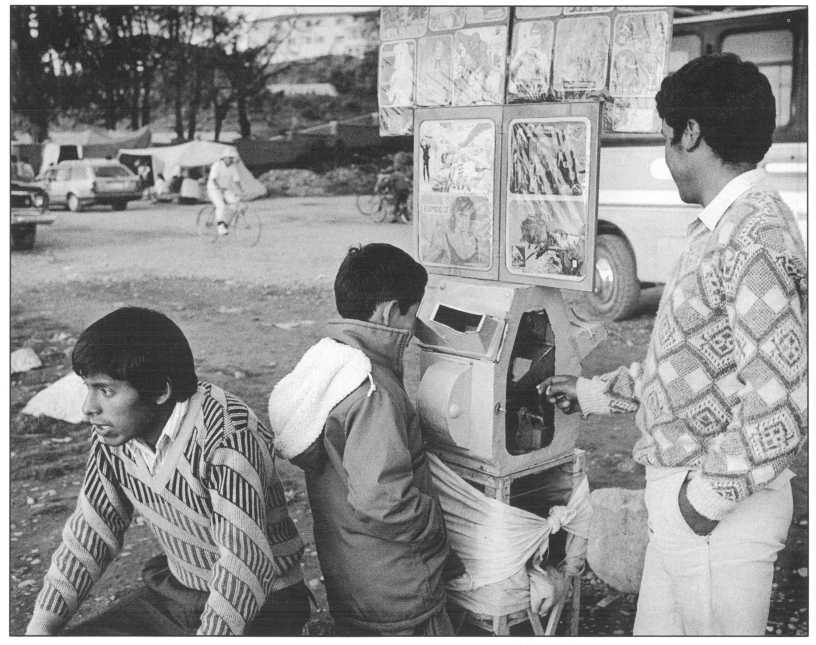

Queueing to view a film in a 'kino-matic' machine, Copacabana, Bolivia

Grinding coffee in Chichicastenango, Guatemala

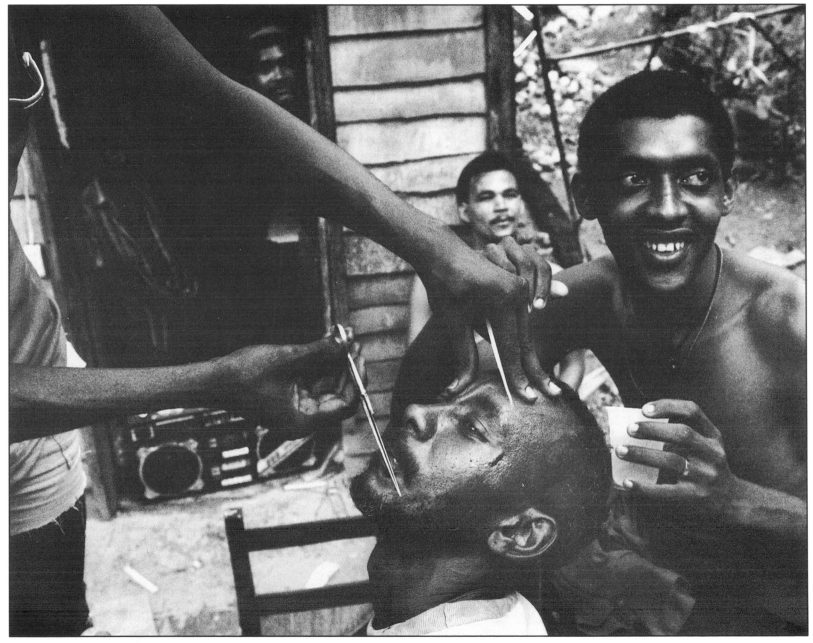

Street barber in a shanty town of Santo Domingo

'It's much better now in Latin America. . .'
'Nothing to worry about. . .'
'Going well. Democracy. Elections. . .'
'Upturn. . .'
'Back on the rails. . .'
'The debt crisis is over. . .'
'Aiming for growth. . .'
'Inflation's being licked. . .'
'The Sandinistas are done for. . .'
'Castro and his men are on their last legs. . .'
'Mexico's OK again. . .'
'The Bank is much happier. . .'
'The Fund has given its good housekeeping seal of approval. . .'
'The first Latin American bonds for years have been issued on the international market. . .'
'The international lenders who had such a hard time in Latin America in the 1980s are putting their toes in the water again. . .'
'I have this deal going in Bolivian paper. . .'

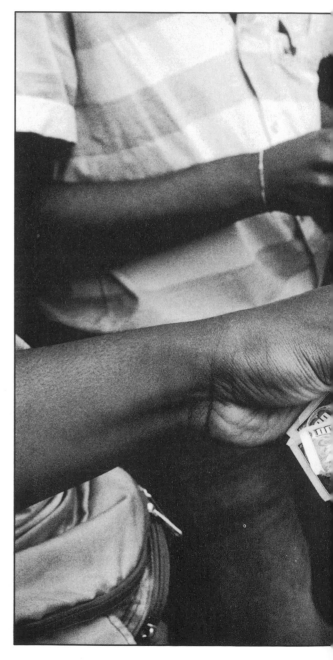

Money changers, Lima, Peru

Hand with mercury, Amazon basin

Goldfish vendor, Rio, Brazil

Panning for gold in the Amazon, Brazil

Herb vendors, Colombia

Market porter, Ecuador

spiritual reunion

moons and mountains

ENRIQUE DUSSEL

When anthropologists see a stone, they see a stone and not a god, so I believe that to keep a god as stone does not destroy it as a god. The Spanish confronted gods, whom they called demons, because they saw how they functioned as living cults, inspiring opposition. They had arrived in the midst of a world of giants. Just think what it must have been like to arrive in Mexico from the Spain of that time: thousands upon thousands, no at least six to eight *million*, people lived in the Valley of Mexico. They were terrified and their fear bred ferocity and so they killed. They believed they were defending themselves or forestalling rebellions. What goes by the name of evangelisation needs to be told from the Indian and not the Spanish standpoint.

An indigenous person saw the resulting battles between armies and temples as drawn from events of the mystical world of the heavens, the grand processions of the sun and the moon and guardians of the days, weeks and months. Each day saw a new procession of gods to whom one had to pay repeated obeisance. We're told that the world to us was a boring place, but there was nothing boring about it. It was perfectly ordered according to consummately important devotions.

So it was that when Spaniards arrived and succeeded in conquering the visible world on behalf of the king and his cohorts, the Indians had to undergo a wholesale conversion, asking themselves: 'Who are these all-powerful gods who have vanquished our gods?' According to their logic they had to enquire, 'Who then is your god? . . . Jesus Christ . . . then let us worship him. Why? . . . Because he has overcome.'

In other words, they were not employing Christian logic but a logic of their own in drawing these conclusions. For example, when a people was conquered, the Spanish burnt all its codices, supposedly in the process of assimilation. Dismembering a rebel into five parts was something that had never happened in Aragon or Castille or anywhere else, yet Coyocatl was torn into five parts. This was the punishment the Spaniard began to impose on a rebellious Indian – only upon an Indian. Why? In order to make a sacrifice in true pre-hispanic style.

What I'm saying is that the Spaniards also entered into an ideology that wasn't native to them. They acted upon it from the moment they arrived. To put it another way, the hispanic vision of the cosmos had to change. By the time Cortés arrived, a biological hecatomb was entered out of which we still haven't found our way – born of his shock at seeing churches disparagingly called stone mountains, up which you could climb for ten metres without a single stone dislodging onto your head. That had a greater teleological impact than their own canonfire.

So the process began immediately. When the twelve missionaries arrived, the indigenous people themselves saw that even the Spaniards afforded the Franciscans considerable respect. This should not be overlooked. For example when Archbishop Torivio Mogrovejo arrived in Lima, the viceroy greatly impressed the Inca by descending from his carriage in order to kiss his feet, since that was the custom in Spain. Thus the indigenous people saw their own viceroy in an act of obeisance before the archbishop and said: 'The archbishop must be more important than any of the others.' It was the archbishop who made a fetish of the temple while the viceroy showed not the slightest interest. According to our beliefs those without religious custom are without authority.

This signifies that the admission of churchmen was integral to this complete transformation of a cosmic vision.

planets and pyramids

JEFE MAYA HUMBATZ MEN

The Spaniards didn't arrive here and announce: 'We shall respect the pyramids and build our churches beside them.' No – and why not? They demolished pyramids in order to impose their churches. That marks a lack of respect . . . and yet certain Christian principles are those of the Maya. 'Love your neighbour as yourself.' That's identical to Latrich Maya's saying: 'You are I and I you.' But if they'd practised what they came to preach, perhaps history would have been different. But that isn't what happened. . .

Now they talk about it in a manner that makes it sound both funny and obscure, making statements to the effect that: 'Of course the Aztecs also imposed their religion on others.' I don't see it like that since no indigenous culture ever arrived and demolished all the pyramids there simply in order to erect their own. On the contrary, if those arriving discovered pyramids in a state of collapse they rebuilt them. And why? Because we believe that the work of human hands is sacred and should not be destroyed. That's why our pyramids are built on a belief of renewal and reconstruction.

Westerners always took the opposite approach. They appeared and tore down and built over. Why did they do that, when what was already there was sacred? . . . According to my analysis of the situation and my researches into our old

books, belonging to a culture doesn't signify a return to the past: it is to understand the nature of time. Our cultures take their inspiration from time and from time's cycles . . . The way we all have to live now means that yes, we've resolved certain problems but we've also broken up a great deal. That's something we have to think over very carefully.

Now we're planning for a Mayan Community, to integrate and work together: we're looking for a way through. Maybe other people accuse us of looking for a way backwards rather than forwards but that won't change our values. And of course we want to live in harmony with the land, the community, 'the people of the light'. . .

Indigenous Andean cultures were integrated into natural law. What happens if we now try to live according to natural laws? Can we make Aids, cancer or any other modern diseases simply disappear? It doesn't work like that.

Of course we want to adhere to natural law, and recognise that the greatest problems of today stem from the fact that human beings have dismantled a whole system of natural laws. And that with its disintegration, there's no longer any respect for those things we hold sacred, like the trees. Transnational companies are devouring all our forests. As the ancient Maya prophecy says: 'The day the last tree

The ancient Maya city of Chichén Itza, for example, was a great political centre and Palenque a great religious centre where the standing stones explain the story of human evolution. Chichén combined the astronomical and the political: its so-called 'castle' perfectly fronts the rising sun as it comes over the coastal horizon. Uxmal is the female centre, its name means 'the feminine plural of the eternal moon', and the female planet is of course the moon, because it governs women's physiological functions.

That's something we find very beautiful, the bond between women and the earth. Nowadays it has become the parallel between the maltreatment of the land and of women, or their social marginalisation ever since the West became our rulers. That involves women's relegation to secondary status and the earth too has been relegated and even raped in the same way as our women were. For us that conforms to our tradition which tells us that woman doesn't just symbolise femininity but also the earth itself, with its connections to fertility, to light. . . Woman belongs to two planets, earth and the moon, whereas man has only one, the sun.

Within our communities, our indigenous societies accord women equal importance to men. Thus Moctezuma, for example, had Ciguacoatz to govern beside him. Man's role was to legislate, woman's to administrate, and so things happened without any of the social problems we have today. There were also councils of elders and of children, and women were integrated at every level, never separated out.

disappears, so does the last human being.' We could add that when we do away with the trees we do away with ecology and we'll all be dead. So yes, there are things we hold as absolute truths and it doesn't particularly matter at what date they happened to be written down.

That indigenous structure is still latent in contemporary Mexican society. That's one reason why sociologists fail to understand how women fought alongside men in the Mexican Revolution [1910-19]. That's a reflection of our ancient ways of organising, women never being left behind.

island magic

MIGENE GONZALEZ-WIPPLER

According to the last US census there were nearly three million Puerto Ricans in the United States in 1990. Approximately one third of them live in New York City. The rest are spread out throughout the country, with large concentrations in Miami, Los Angeles and San Francisco.

The lives of most Latin Americans – not only Puerto Ricans – are intrinsically linked to magical and spiritual beliefs. Even though they avow a total commitment to Christianity in general, and Catholicism in particular, latinos feel quite comfortable with the practice of *espiritismo*, or communication with the dead through mediumnistic trances, and *santería* – the Afro-Cuban religion with roots in Southwestern Nigeria.

Espiritismo was made popular in Latin America through the books of the French spiritualist Hippolyte Léon Dénizard Rivail, better known under the pseudonym of Alain Kardec. Since Kardec's books were brought to Latin America as contraband in the late nineteenth century, his ideas and philosophy spread like wild fire throughout the various Latin American countries, in spite of its highly vocal condemnation of the Catholic Church. In the United States, notably New York, many *centros espiritistas* or 'spiritist' temples have sprung up throughout the inner cities. The centres are headed by a president and several principal mediums, one of whom is often his wife. They are supported by membership fees and voluntary donations. Their main activities are séances conducted around a white-covered table. The various mediums help establish contact between the *centro*'s clients and their departed loved ones. The mediums also give advice on personal problems; exorcise houses and businesses; divine the future with Tarot cards; conduct spiritual purifications and sometimes cast spells – all for a pre-arranged fee.

But perhaps the most prevalent magical practice among Puerto Ricans and other latinos in the United States is that of *santería*. Brought to the country by exiled Cubans after Castro took over, *santería* is a syncretic religion that blends some of the magico-religious beliefs and practices of the Yoruba people with some tenets of the Catholic Church. The identification of Catholic saints with some of the Yoruba deities – known as *orishas* – is the most significant aspect of this Afro-Cuban religion and is the reason why it is called *santería*, the worship of saints.

The popularity of *santería* is due partly to its great emphasis on rituals and magic. The *santero* – or priest – is an expert herbalist, a consummate diviner, and a master magician. He is also a great psychotherapist who is able to assuage his client's fears and doubts with the right mixture of natural magic and common sense. His consultation starts with a divination ritual that can involve the reading of sixteen cowrie shells, the *diloggun*, or four pieces of coconut, the *biague*. What makes his consultation so special is that he does not claim to read the future. He is only the interpreter of an oracle presided over by one of the deities in the Yoruba pantheon, syncretised as a Catholic saint. The saint or *orisha* that presides over the *diloggun* is an ambivalent force known as *eleggua*, who is said to stand at every crossroads and to open and close every door. According to the *santeros* it is imperative to keep *eleggua* happy because he can bring triumph or disaster to each life. This may be effected through offerings favoured by the *orisha*.

Through the divination system known as the *diloggun*, the *santero* tells his client not only the origin of his problems but also how these problems can best be solved. Invariably, possible solutions include ways through which the client may propitiate the saint who has agreed to help solve his/her problems. Although *eleggua* presides over the *diloggun*, he may not necessarily be the saint who undertakes the solution of a given difficulty. One of the most fascinating aspects of *santería* is that every human endeavour is overseen by a particular saint or *orisha*. Love, marriage and money are all ruled by an enchanting deity known as *Oshún*, goddess of river waters. Matters relating to employment, war, as well as surgical procedures, the police, railways, accidents and explosions are governed by an imposing deity known as *Oggun*. The reason why he governs so many disparate elements is that he is the patron saint of metals, which is the one common denominator in all these fields. On the other hand, peace, purity and creativity are ruled by *Obatala*; while fire, power over enemies and passion are governed by the indomitable *Chango*, the thunder god and one of the saints most often invoked. Therefore it is the saint or *orisha* who

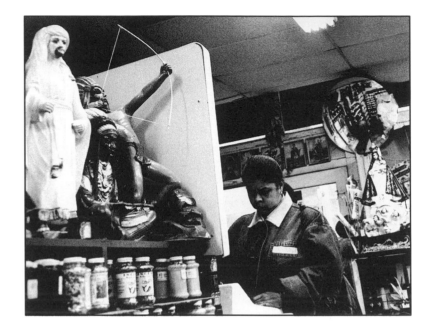

controls the problem faced by the client, who is usually invoked to solve it.

Santería functions through a priesthood of both men and women who have undergone a series of progressive initiations believed to confer special powers on the initiates, as well as the protection of the saints.

Central to the practice of *santería* are the *tambores*, or drum parties, in honour of the saints. Most frequently, drum parties follow a major initiation, when a priest or priestess is ordained. During the *tambores*, saints or *orishas* 'come down' to earth and take possession of some of their initiates. During possession, a person will take on the characteristics associated with a particular deity. The person thus possessed displays exceptional physical strength, an uncanny ability to foresee the future and other supernatural powers. He or she enters the trance through the repetitive rhythm of the drums and the chanting of those present. The drums and chanting act together to induce a deep hypnotic state during which some of the archetypal contents of the deep unconscious surface in the conscious personality, totally overwhelming it. These psychic elements then manifest as the concentrations of power known as *orishas* or saints.

The drums used in *santería* are known as the *bataa*; they originated in Nigeria, the country of the Yoruba people. Every drum that came from Africa carries inside it a kola nut, believed to be the soul of the drum. For that reason each drum was considered to be 'alive', speaking in a voice of its own. The importance of the *bataa* in modern percussion cannot be overemphasised. There is no drum rhythm in Latin music, jazz, rock 'n' roll, or any type of music using percussion that does not exist in the *bataa*. It is at the root of all percussion and is believed to encompass the unified souls of all the gods. That is why the *bataa* is magical and can link the human soul with the divine, through the phenomenon of possession.

Drum parties are communal affairs where people air their problems openly, using the presence of the saints as a safety valve. It is quite common during a *tambor* to hear someone discuss very delicate, intimate problems with the person allegedly possessed by an *orisha*, even in front of a roomful of people. Everyone sympathises with the client, who does not feel in the least embarrassed by the presence of others during this exchange with the *orisha*. The experience is not unlike that of group therapy, and indeed many psychologists have compared the practice of *santería* to a primitive but effective form of psychotherapy.

Puerto Ricans and Cubans have traditionally been close. They seem to empathise with each other more than with other Latin American groups perhaps through the similarity of their cultures. Even their flags are almost identical, with only the colours reversed. Maybe for that reason Puerto Ricans

have embraced *santería* with the same enthusiasm with which they have embraced other traditional Cuban exports, such as the rumba and the mambo. By contrast, people from the neighbouring Dominican Republic are not as interested in *santería* as Puerto Ricans are. This may be because Santo Domingo shares the island of Hispaniola with Haiti, and the powerful influence of Haitian voodoo has long been felt among Dominicans.

But how does one practise Caribbean magic in the asphalt jungles of American cities? How do centuries of magical tradition endure under the harsh climate of modern thought and modern technology? Most important of all, where do the practitioners of *espiritismo*, *santería* and related 'witchcraft' find the ingredients for their rites and spells? In many American cities, such as New York and Miami, the answer can be found in the religious goods stores known as *botánicas*.

A *botánica* is a magical free-for-all, a potpourri of traditions, customs, legends and mysticism. In a well-stocked *botánica* one can find snake skins and oil, powdered deer horn, musk and civet in oil and powder form, dried smoked possum, palm-nut oil, mandrake, asafoetida, betel nuts, cocoa butter, alum powder, centipede-, shark- and turtle oils, as well as the barks, leaves, roots and flowers of hundreds of tropical trees. Every conceivable oil, perfume and magical essence can also be found in the *botánica*, together with natural remedies for every ailment from alcoholism and impotence to cancer and chronic bronchitis. Stones, talismans, candles, incenses and images of the saints are also found in the *botánicas*, where every item, however small, has magical significance.

Botánicas have become so popular that they are quickly being integrated into the latino scene in large American cities. They are the main supply source for *espiritismo*, *santería* and other magical practices. In recent years, the *botánica* business has grown to such an extent that many tons of herbs and roots and a variety of botanical products are imported weekly from neighbouring Latin American countries, notably Puerto Rico and the Dominican Republic. Therefore the economies of these countries are being helped by the practice of Caribbean magic in the United States. Furthermore, because of the increasing influx of other Latin American nationals to the United States, the magical scenario is widening and now Colombians, Venezuelans, Argentines, Ecuadorians, Peruvians, Guatemalans, and other South and Central Americans are practising *espiritismo* and *santería* in American cities. This has led to a fascinating intercultural phenomenon. Because many of these immigrants eventually return – permanently or temporarily – to their country of origin, they import syncretic magico-religious beliefs to their native lands. The result is that *espiritismo, santería*, and other allied practices are now found in parts of Latin America where they were almost unknown several years ago. Even Spain is feeling the call of the magical siren and many *santeros* travel periodically to Spanish cities to conduct initiations and other ritual ceremonies for wealthy Spaniards who are *santería* practitioners.

Still more interesting, the magical practices of latinos in the US are catching the attention of both white and black Americans, who have begun to show a deepening interest in their practices. *Santería* is particularly popular, and many North Americans are joining the ranks of the *santería* priesthood. Therefore, in a curious way, Caribbean magic is becoming a way of life, a new spiritual awakening in the United States, and a search for soul roots, found in the atavistic rhythms of the drums and the powers of the saints.

Making offerings at a santería ritual, Havana, Cuba

Police and Roman soldiers, Good Friday, Arcos, Spain

The Resurrection

From the dust of the Araucanians
from the stone of the Aztecs
from the blood of the slaves
comes the resurrection.
Let butterflies catch fire
let the wind then seize them
to ignite the volcano
and give hymn to the thunder.
The sun is hoisted
from its dawning dreams
that howl on awakening
to the dead's great gathering.

Dust on dust
stone on stone
out of their faces
a city arises,
The ancient mountain chain
casts its spell,
the wind blows sharply
singing of freedom.
The warriors return
to the cry of the earth.

African drums partly hiding the Holy Heart of Christ, Cuba

Drummer playing candombe at the Montevideo carnivals, Uruguay

Previous contact is essential for whatever type of possession. The person gifted to be chosen as one possessed by a saint, to truly assume their gestures and character, at once acquires a powerful status within whichever social nucleus these practices find a home. It's worth underlining that this status ranks as much in the social sphere as in the religious.

Dancing by an outdoor altar, Havana, Cuba

Let us invoke the Heart of the Heavens and
the Heart of the Earth that they light the way
to fraternity and unity among our indigenous
Peoples.

Let it dawn
may the first light come
that people may live in peace,
great peace and joy,
and grant us a good life
a worthy existence.

That we all may rise up,
that we all may be called,
that there be no different peoples
among us all,
who stay behind the rest.

Grant us our descendants
as you granted us our ancestors,
for as long as the sun revolves
and light returns.

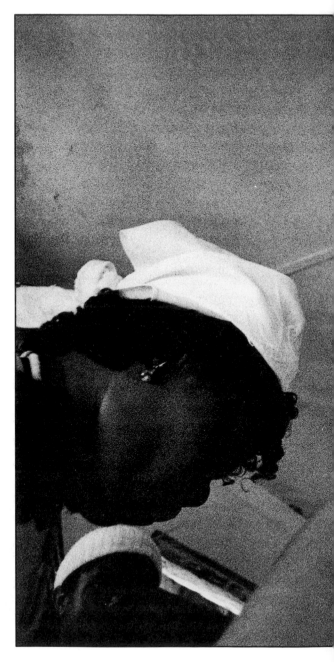

Woman in a trance at a santería session, Marianao, Havana, Cuba

If ever the devil were to emerge, he would appear here in these mines. Here, we would expect to find him at his fiercest and clearest. The amounts extracted from the earth by far exceeded anything under the Inca; yet at *the top of the ladder* the Indians met only further indebtedness, while the ore was removed to Spanish coffers. There was neither the material nor the spiritual repayment necessary to overcome the traumas inflicted on the mountain gods, traumas that by their sheer and senseless size would overwhelm the recuperative powers of any traditional ritual. Virtually nothing returned to the miners, or to their gods, to whom the Indians, as much as all of surrounding nature, were beholden. The indigenous world was riddled by the destructive powers of the universe that had been unleashed from their moorings at the beginning of the exchange. The totality was split at every point.

Dancers with 'armadillo', Oruro, Bolivia

Funeral drums at a santería altar, Cuba

Dance of the Liberation of the Slaves, National Folk Group, Cuba

Hooded man. Holy Week, Arcos, Spain

Altar of our Virgin of Socavón, Oruro, Bolivia

The Empty Church

The church is empty now:
no children yelling,
no guitars strumming.
Nature alone takes note of what is happening
*   there.*
The grass will grow again as before,
the wind and the rain will lash the flowering
*   palm-tree,*
birds will come and eat mangos,
swallows will still build their nests
in the eaves of the church.
Now only the flowers and the song of the birds
can bring joy in the silent days.

Hooded children, Arcos, Spain

Burning incense at Chichicastenango, Guatemala

Aymara family lighting candles at Copacabana on Lake Titicaca, Bolivia

Let there be no animosity in our hearts. Let the Eucharist, this call to reconciliation with God and our brothers and sisters, leave the imprint of Christianity in all our hearts. . . Let us pray for the conversion of those who strike us. . . of those who sacrilegiously dare touch the holy tabernacle. Let us pray to the Lord for forgiveness and for the due repentance of those who turned this town into a prison and a torture chamber. Let the Lord touch their hearts. Before the terrible sentence is accomplished – 'he that kills by the sword will also die by the sword.' Let them truly repent and have the satisfaction of looking on him they have pierced. And may there rain from there a torrent of mercy and kindness, so we may all feel ourselves to be brothers and sisters.

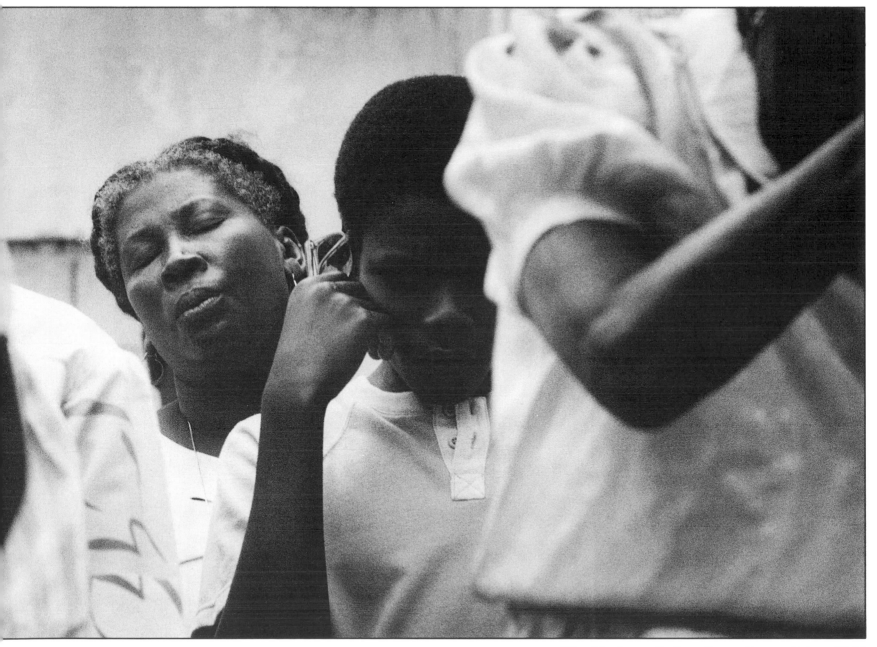

Worshipping at St. Jean Bosco, Port au Prince, Haiti

Trumpets at the diablada carnival in Oruro, Bolivia

Quechua fishermen on Lake Titicaca, Peru

references

p. 29: Fidel Castro, *Revolución*, 7 September 1961

pp. 32, 35: Gilberto Dimenstein, *Brazil: War on Children*

p. 39: Ana María Condori (with Inneke Dibbits and Elizabeth Peredo), *Nayan Unatatawi/Mi Despertar*

p. 52: José Comas, 'La Transformación del señor presidente,' *El País Internacional*, 1 June 1987. Quoted in James Ferguson, *Dominican Republic: Beyond the Lighthouse*

p. 53: By the Chilean poet in exile Maria Eugenia Bravo. Translated by Dinah Livingstone and Amanda Hopkinson

p. 57: Paco Sol, 'En Defensa de los Tacos,' *El Grito: a Journal of Contem-porary Mexican American Thought*, 1986

p. 60: Salman Rushdie, *The Jaguar Smile: a Nicaraguan Journey*

p. 82: David Yanomani, 'Creation Myths of the Yanomani People,' in *Survival International Newsletter*, no. 27 1990

p. 89: Interview by Julio Etchart with Father Aristide, President of Haiti now in exile, Port au Prince, May 1991

p. 90: Michael T. Taussig, *The Devil and Commodity Fetishism in South America*

p. 92: Ta' Lorando, José Luis Guerra, a candombe recorded by the Uruguayan group Los Olimarenos

p. 95: Oscar Hijuelos, *Our House in the Last World*

p. 97: Juan Goytisolo, *Landscapes After the Battle*

p. 111: Interview with Juan Diego, fire eating among the traffic on Avenida Reforma

p. 112: Graham Greene, *The Comedians*

p. 117: Ciro Alegría, *Broad and Alien is the World*

p. 122: Hugh O'Shaughnessy, 'The Debt Crisis'

p. 141: By Silvio Rodríguez. Quoted in Heinz Dieterich Steffan (ed), *(1492–1992: La Interminable Conquista*, tr. A. Hopkinson

p. 142: Miguel Barnet, 'La Santería Cubana,' unpublished lecture, 1991

p. 144: Que amenezca llegue la autora...! From the Maya Chilam Balam

p. 147: Bernabé Cobo, *Historia del Nuevo Mundo*

p. 151: *The Peasant Poets of Solentíname*, tr. Peter Wright

p. 154: Archbishop Romero's last homily. Quoted in James Brockman, *Oscar Romero, Bishop and Martyr*